PENNILESS POLITICS

Also by Douglas Oliver

Oppo Hectic (Ferry Press, 1969)
The Harmless Building (Grosseteste and Ferry Presses, 1973)
In the Cave of Suicession (Street Editions, 1974)
The Diagram Poems (Ferry Press, 1979)
The Infant and the Pearl (Silver Hounds for Ferry Press, 1985)
Kind: Collected Poems (Allardyce, Barnett, Publishers, 1987)
Poetry and Narrative in Performance (Macmillan/St Martin's Press, 1989)
Three Variations on the Theme of Harm (Paladin, 1990)
The Scarlet Cabinet, with Alice Notley (Scarlet Editions, NY, 1992)

PENNILESS POLITICS

A SATIRICAL POEM BY
DOUGLAS OLIVER

BLOODAXE BOOKS

Copyright © Douglas Oliver 1991, 1992, 1994

ISBN: 1 85224 269 8

This edition first published 1994 by
Bloodaxe Books Ltd,
P.O. Box 1SN,
Newcastle upon Tyne NE99 1SN.

Bloodaxe Books Ltd acknowledges
the financial assistance of Northern Arts.

LEGAL NOTICE

All rights reserved. No part of this book may be
reproduced, stored in a retrieval system, or
transmitted in any form, or by any means, electronic,
mechanical, photocopying, recording or otherwise,
without prior written permission from Bloodaxe Books Ltd.

Requests to publish work from this book
must be sent to Bloodaxe Books Ltd.

Douglas Oliver has asserted his right under
Section 77 of the Copyright, Designs and Patents Act 1988
to be identified as the author of this work.

Cover printing by J. Thomson Colour Printers Ltd, Glasgow.

Printed in Great Britain by
Cromwell Press Ltd, Broughton Gifford, Melksham, Wiltshire.

*Dedicated to the poets of the Lower East Side,
New York City, and to the community of
St Mark's Place, who showed me much kindness
during my nearly five years' residence there.
I never said I didn't love New York.*

ACKNOWLEDGEMENTS

Penniless Politics was first published in 1991 by Iain Sinclair's Hoarse Commerce (London) as an interim publication in a limited edition of 200 copies. It was reprinted by Scarlet Editions (New York City) in 1992 as part of *The Scarlet Cabinet*, a compendium of books by Alice Notley and Douglas Oliver. The poem has been revised for this new edition from Bloodaxe.

Howard Brenton's Foreword was first published as a review of the original Hoarse Commerce edition of the poem in *The Guardian* on 7 April 1992. Thanks are due to Howard Brenton and Guardian Newspapers Limited for their kind permission to reprint the article.

The illustration on page 9 is a *vèvè* for voodoo goddess Erzulie, taken from *Le vaudou haitien* by Alfred Métraux (TEL Gallimard, 1968).

CONTENTS

11   *Foreword* by HOWARD BRENTON

15   Part 1
37   Part 2
51   Part 3

80   *Biographical note*

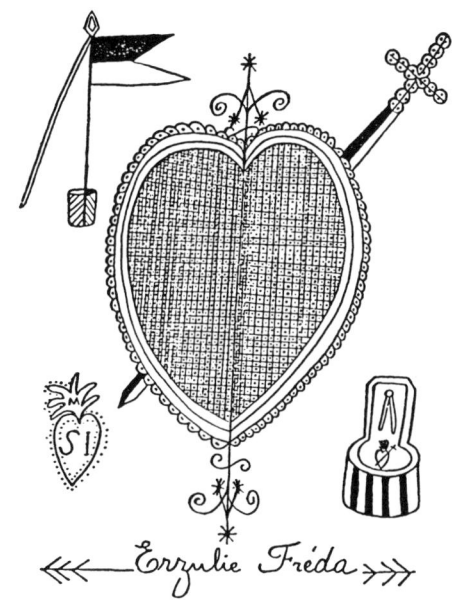

FOREWORD

What was the shock like, reading T.S. Eliot's *The Waste Land* when it was published in 1922? I think I know. I've just read Douglas Oliver's epoch-making long poem, *Penniless Politics*. I never thought I would ever read anything like it in the 1990s. *Penniless Politics* sets the literary agenda for the next 20 years.

Douglas Oliver is, from what 'the poet' says of himself in the text, white and an 'Anglo-Scot' living as an outsider near a wrecked district of Manhattan, where the poem is set. He is wonderfully bloody-minded; his great poem is at the moment only available in a curious samizdat edition.

As with Eliot's masterpiece, Oliver's poem will divide friends. I had a furious argument with an old leftie about it: 'How can you think this is poetry? What's all this about voodoo? It's repugnant! Pseudo art, pseudo politics…You'll be a laughing-stock if you praise this garbage.' I fear Douglas Oliver is going to need a heavyweight champion, as did Eliot; no doubt his F.R. Leavis will appear.

Bizarrely, the poem's plot resembles the old British film *Passport to Pimlico*, though Ealing comedy it ain't. A poor district of New York declares 'UDI', reinventing politics from the ground, indeed from the groin, upwards – the sex in the poem is terrific.

'To begin with everything missing…' says the second stanza. And from a heady brew of voodoo notions of spirit, curious visitations of communal inspirations, democratic seances, a melt-down of old politics, grassroots scams and 'buy-ups' of neighbourhoods, a political movement stirs among the poor of New York and 'District A1' is born, a truly free zone. It thrives, then in a second disappears, its 'spirit' aged. For how are politics possible in the Utopian dreams of a poem? This is a diamond-hard mind talking to us:

> What did you expect? You, hypocrite reader,
> et cetera? You want some opiate, a poetic abracadabra
> so your ordinary responsibility for our ordinary political failure
> can be charmed away?

The poem is, formally, a satire, a 'criticism in verse of folly and vice'. But its attack on late 20th century America is startlingly original. Rather than attempt to ridicule things as they are, as *Bonfire of the Vanities* failed to do since no fictional New York folly can exceed the outrage of the real thing, Oliver turns the negativity of satire on its head. He does so by describing his imaginary, alternative America with a blazing optimism. A crazed but certain faith that human invention could transform the New York urban nightmare surges through the poem's 300 or more eight-lined, elaborately rhymed and rhythmed stanzas, white-hot with linguistic energy, coining poetic devices with abandon. The poem even includes a new US Constitution.

And there is the authentic beauty of Oliver's city writing. Try this description of a market:

> As cabbage leaves drift on the sidewalk and cherries, squashed, bleep
> their stones, ice sparkles under broccoli, the washed beans seep
> water through slats of wood out at Hunt's Point, and it's only 6.30,
> the wholesale market already almost done, the rest of the city
> barely waking as the dawn gleams on unsold boxes of onions,
> the trucks in circles like cowboy wagons...

As great writing will, *Penniless Politics* identifies a new era's theme that we all sense to be there, just beyond language, waiting for its first expression. The poem's theme is desire: a ferocious, overwhelming desire for the human spirit to change. It is hard to imagine anything more unfashionable, for we're not meant to be able to believe in 'changing the world'; but then the poem is way beyond the pale of what is, for the moment, acceptable as literature, or as political or moral thought. Could it be that the most unlikely thing, a *poem*, can show the way out of the post-communist, post-modernist, 'ideas are dead' miasma that is poisoning us? I suggest the reader hold on and take the rollercoaster ride through Oliver's amazing plot and the dizzying heights and water splashes of his poetic invention. It's worth it because the poem, with its ambitious-as-Milton first line –

All politics the same crux: to define humankind richly.

– to its blistering final stanzas, could well be our *Paradise Lost*.

HOWARD BRENTON

PENNILESS POLITICS

A Satirical Poem

PART 1

All politics the same crux: to define humankind richly.
No one non-populist or penniless can found a viable party
though most religions have such saints. She was his Haitian
saint Emen – Emen for Marie-Noelle – for non-Christian
Mary-Christmas. In New York with him, her husband, Will Penniless,
they'll found their party in a poem. Black with White nation,
Voodoo-Haitian with immigrant Anglo-Scots, hairy-chesty,
penniless, Mrs Penniless, with him, Will Penniless.

To begin with everything missing. Emen set aside contempt
for extreme right or left, mein kampf or ill-kempt
politicians, or for middle-roaders. She held fire. 'If we got married
all might be overcome,' said Will hopefully, knowing their road
had to start absolutely from rough ground, not a track behind them,
just doves crowding trees black with starlings, white bird
between each black one. Their first steps aimed to pre-empt
mimicry of the past, to enter silence, then put it behind them.

Their poet has a white male face just as mean as each face
of rich white males in today's *Post*: the New York Mayor race.
So though he may tell he may not star in the story, outlawed
from penniless power. He (Will) tells how that day, bored,
Emen asked Will, 'Do we have to get married?' Who replied, 'For you,
power may grow by separation. But we whites are so flawed
that we must change sexually too. You decide.' 'For your race
I'll marry this once. And for love I'll make Voodoo for you.'

As Will and Emen tumble down through their love, he'll
keep telling their story impersonally. Sex needs such tact. They'll
always know she opened Will's eyes one morning in Brooklyn,
Utica Avenue; on their marital bed she, the Haitian,
changed his skin sympathies, unshackled his stiff pelvis
by mounting him, squirting black womanly sperm into him,
remaking his mind and his tongue while he was still
asleep, new conceptions warm and liquid in his pelvis.

The opening of eyes, changing of person, exchange of sexes,
Black for White, We for They, Woman on Top, all this is
not merely antithesis: lying on his back, Will gazed
up at Emen's eyes browsing as if he were a book while she grazed
his lips with Haitian lips, her hips working
at his hips, on his chest her breasts drifting cloudily sideways.
He felt male, white, but so much gave up his penis
to Emen that it could have been hers in him, working.

She sat above him on her altar there. Finished. Like her mother
once, a U.S. voodoo mambo retired to Ouanaminthe, crooning to Legba:
'*Attibon Legba, ouvri bayé pour moin,*' open the wicket
to the spirit world. '*Ago! Ou wé,*' you see me at the gate,
open it for me. '*Ouvri bayé pour moin, ouvri bayé.*' Hear
the call to Legba, Will, '*M'apé rentré lo ma tourné.*' Will wait,
'I will enter when I return'. Praise him, Will, '*Ma salut loa
yo!*' In origin male or female, red clay, Legba's old phallus here.

They talked of a Haitian memory: rare rains had caked the savannah
plateau as they travelled south from seeing maman
at Ouanaminthe on the Dom Rep border; they sat, stranded, shaken
by truck rides, beside the few huts, the Belgian mission
of St. Raphael, crossroads in flatlands, their rice and beans
bought from a householder; in the backdrop each black mountain
patched with erosion's tarpaulins; this for Will a true Legba-
like moment, recalling Port-au-Prince slums, the kids lacking beans.

Under Nature's blind eyes, on Earth's body, Emen drew the congo cross
of souls circling criss-cross of living and dead. Heterodox,
Emen took a political vow with Will there, since maman mambo,
orthodox, had scorned their wedding, and added: 'I told you no:
I lived there: I was a *boat people* in a land of baseballs.
Her religion's Yankee politics. Mine's true to *noirisme*, voodoo.
My poor *pays terrifié*, suffering so bad from Papa Doc's
pouvoir baroniel, and now our poor make your country's baseballs!

'What matters,' maman had snarled, rounding the mid-pole of her *hounfor*
by the Massacre River, 'is how wide (*large*) you're thinking before
you begin.' Emen had made an oath: 'Let us live on the margin
of life and death, world citizens before our national origin,
unsexed before sexed, poor before rich. A great bowl fills a bucket
through a hole in the bottom, the world fills the domestic, women
fill men, magic fills the rational.' This became what they swore
by the St. Raphael huts where 'wealth' was pink and slimy in a bucket.

Dawn there. Worrying burble of dawn chorus quietening. Dull.
A cloudy nowhere. Yet political. No sound now. Already political.
Pink light behind closed eyelids. In Will's blindness her brown hand
drawing a *vèvè*, the sacred figure, drawing with flour on to sand,
a simple cross on a St. Raphael path, white on brown, Legba
the Voodoo crossroads loa; in silence they were going beyond
pantheons and had trod out that single path to the simple
cross-stroke, first political choice, sign of Legba.

The *vèvè* scintillated at its cross-point, a glint of fire
issuing from an ant-hole in the inert silicon, a power
that transcends naming by priestcraft, not Allah's oneness,
nor Guatama's enlightenment, nor unity of trinity, nor singleness
at the heart of any four-fold-truth or of four ends of humans,
nor therefore finally Legba's own fire, not a loa's prowess
but something obvious to all, a grand cliché: higher
knowing includes birth of action; at crossroads we become humans.

In the tiny flame's center the idea of their party was found.
Exactly in, not round it. They stepped inside there. Flames around
their embrace. Brotherly... sisterly... but also the sexual
flame inaugurates the political. Sweeted by flame they fell
down a chute of memory, partly personal but also transforming
the personal into memory held by whole peoples; central, central,
get central and you'll fall down that chute, flames, a dark
descent into conception, blindness of ideas transforming.

Beside Brooklyn's pale windows they reaffirmed Haiti, their apartment
a telephone receiver shape. Up on Utica, the brick tenement
looked downhill long past Carib cafes, bodegas, the Santeria
botanica where Emen bought plaster saints, down to shadier
Prospect Park; wind swept white doves off branches; starlings:
black dice thrown a moment. Trembling as if Legba possessed her:
'You've got to join my spirits before we talk of government.'
White doves skirting out in fear then flocking to the starlings.

Naked brown and whitey-pink, they walked through their apartment
on Utica and, arm round her, Will warned: 'You can't make government
from religious spirit.' The room full of charms, a St. John
statue at his knee, thunder loa stone, wall blankets, the Oshun
chiming bracelets beside steaming coffee. 'Political theory,'
she smiled, 'splits the world one way, and religion
splits it the other. We'll not mean more than we know and we'll invent
the unexpected, free of priestcraft, messianism, masculine theory.'

That morning they drafted their first manifesto, not in verse.
They looked in the jar: twenty dollars, a few cents, worse,
the phone cut off and a pizza to buy for lunch. Will put carbon-
layered sheets into his Olivetti and typed a little. '*Ah bon!*'
exclaimed Emen. 'Now add this, oh and this, and this,'
as the keys rattled and a fuzzy document emerged from the ribbon.
'Chain letters!' blurted Will. 'That will get over the curse
of poverty!' After retyping, the document read like this:

Dear Dolores:

The U.S. has room for a political party twice the size of the tired old Republicans and Democrats. Less than half the American people vote – easily the lowest turnout of any major Western democracy. Just add it up: 40 million missing voters or many more if everyone registered. A new political party could swamp an election. And it's going to be simpler to start one than you ever believed, so simple we're doing it by chain letter.

Photocopy this and send it to three of your friends – preferably ones who don't normally vote. Then come to the Memorial Day Center, 13th Street, on September 14. All questions about the new party will be answered then. We, the undiscovered political America, will make sure it's something we *can* vote for.

Sincerely,

EMEN AND WILL

Take that prose and I'll...Let music take the prose and I'll
tell some real thing, giving the fictional melody and muscle
as 20 Hispanic and Black women bunch underneath the day
center's stage, 13th Street, and a massive Afro-Cuban who may
not stay, being the only male besides Will, and somehow does.
Emen at the mike says: 'Some of you think there's not so many
of us, but we only wanted 20 and thought probably female,
and here's a second man. Look at his size! He's tremendous!'

Emen sparked like static in her store-bought dress, gleaming brown
in buttercup yellow, hips perched on gold-painted pumps, downtown
strut across stage light shining from fierce excitement tight
and controlled. 'Yes, Mr Magnifico Cuban, *gwo neg*, you a right-
wing refugee? All *my* brothers sent back at sea. You get resident
status easy?' The man grinned like a bison. 'Just wanted to fight
for money, Ma'am. Ain't no professional fights on Cuba. I come aroun'
tonight to hear how you're goin' to give us our next pee-resident.'

Emen: 'I'll name you now...name you High John, a long and knotty tap root.
Yessan my thoughts tie up in knots, my words'll untie the knot.
Listen to me girls, listen to me John, listen to me Will,
we're starting way in our minds behind the politicians. What'll
they do for us? D'you see East River swirling chemical
past our lives? White man sells a normal, sells a normal
condo: we're gonna drum a normal, drum a normal congo.
How does the song go? We all learnt it long ago
the hard way: ses sold on the corner, crack at Prospect Park.

Gonna drive through, senator? Don't stroll there in the dark,
shadow over neighborhoods, your cartop movie
of clouds wiped black by bridges; coasting along, senator, groovy, poverty
only half visible, but evil all around. Do you get the vibes?
Car phone rings, another builder offering bribes.
In the toy war of your politics it's who has that ringing tone,
who gets stuck in craters sleeping on their own.
Behoooold this Brooklyn school, just trying to advance,
dirty feet itchy in old socks shuffling into the Regents
exam; and the school board dubious...
Does that make you furious?
Those politico horsemouths open and swallow the wind
while their high-rise projects suck our children
into elevators pungent with poverty. We're gonna put our sex
into estate management and City Hall won't guess what happens next.
You ought to see my new mind
new children alive there from microsecond to microsecond
and the wider winds rise in fury
us, us, supremely now the jury
sitting down in judgment on a loss of nationhood
we women with our bodies of light and blood
no longer on the doorstep making what we scrub
clean rise in price, no longer the soft-shelled crab
creeping into their kneeling buses, victims of the soft sell,
the hardness power of an exploding city. Well,
no law against making half a city highly moneyed
but we're going to make it spiritually honeyed
for behoooold the grim order reaper waiting for our lives
while lawyers and medicos store our honey in their hives.
Race, race, race, prunes supposed to hate the milk,
milk souring, greed, graft, greed, white talk
souring. We're going to eat Black food, my honeys, taste the snake;
we'll be Ayida-Weda's daughters; we'll take a trick
or two from Legba the trickster, even if you're Catholics
or whatever your sense of the sacred, you Hispanics,
or godless like Will, my husband dear, who tries so hard
to have dark consciousness though dressed in his leopard
spotty skin. As yet, don't ask me, we don't have a *program*.
Who d'you think I am? An economist, a law-maker? Don't be absurd,
High John. Let's put the serpent back in the sky. Politics
will come once we recreate spirit; then we'll talk *program*.'

High John thrust fist in air, captivated by the active haunches
of the buttercup Haitian striding there; he rode her vocal punches
with 'Awwight!'; otherwise grinned like a bear now, mute.
Fat and busy Dolores, at 50 unable to pay for her first heart
pacemaker, got irritated at male-ficarum and climbed the stage.
She fluttered black mackerel hue of Hispanic eyelids, her salute
fist contra fist to the Cuban, meaning 'You're out to many lunches',
as she said...but I'll enter her mind not her words at this stage.

I come over from Morrisania section, South Bronx, a bit
of Santeria here, Catholic there, great danger this room gets lit
up by flimflam. Don't be too smart: fool sees corruption
and hates the whole thing; police bad: hate policing; politician
bad: hate governing; monopoly stores bad: steal their produce;
until we live among and are thieves. City housing departments? I mention
'honest' up there I'm called naive. I been pitching it
to them a hundred years; no result for puertorriqueno, can't produce

the *quid pro quo*, they say. D'you think my *barrio* don't know
'bout powerlessness? Morrisania, just tops for living below
the poverty line with income support, public assistance, 46 per cent.
plus...medicaid, supplemental security: citywide only 17 per cent.
Vacant lots 39.1 per cent.; citywide 7.5... 'Verna Lee Judge,
70, clearing wine bottles from the sidewalk.' The per cent.
of AIDS deaths double the city's... Dolores spoke: 'You
gonna do a little *brujo*, little spell here or somping? Judge

for yourself, Emen. Who gonna listen? Sure, you look right pretty
up here, but try being dumpy, hunchback, chipmunk-eyed in this city
like me...' She grinned wide and whirled round to show her plump rump.
'You gonna take out full page ads like billionaire Donald Trump?
I tell you how to go to work. First we tell plenty lies, make trouble
until everyone say 'Hey! Whass going on?' We gotta bump
up the action, start us a little newspaper, get publicity,
dream a little trouble, make more, keep on troubling, no end to trouble.'

From the floor, Will: 'Our friend Dolores is celebrated
for championing her, er, *barrio*, Morrisania. But let's not get hated
like the city bureaucracy. We have to spread out from the, er, Tao
of immediate neighborhood, of ourselves doing good, into
an honest politics engaged in the wider good. How can lies
be the best beginning?' Emen answered him: 'Put these two
views together, call the lies cheap tricks to get the poor started;
later appoint party honesty-functionaries to see where truth lies.'

Dolores again: 'It will need a few bucks to succeed with my plan,
for first this center's custodian needs a bribe; and then
you'll all go out tonight, infesting the neighborhood with rumor
invented by me. Next, find me some trashy block newspaper
too local to know me, too small to check a freelance story,
and Will, you can rewrite my English. *The Brooklyn Blazer?*
Just right: only other editors read it!' It was the Cuban
who came up with cash; they got busy; so now read their story:

VOODOO'D VOTERS SWARM TO NEWEST U.S. PARTY

POLS WHO WORK BY MAGIC

The leaders of Spirit, a new political party, denied today that a Voodoo spell brought the public flocking to their first open meeting.

A surprise turnout of 900 packed a small day care center in Brooklyn after attractive Haitian, Mrs Emen Penniless, daughter of a Voodoo priestess, sent out a single chain letter only two weeks before the meeting. The letter urged recipients to send further letters asking friends and strangers to go to the event.

Bronx Hispanic radical, Dolores Esteves, charged that Mrs Penniless, well-known for her Voodoo practices, could only have raised such support by casting a spell.

'My envelope had herbs in it, and Emen's husband admitted that there were certain rites performed, though he wouldn't tell me what.'

Emen retorted that Dolores was miffed because her own years of activism had failed to draw the crowds. 'It's just plain tomfoolery,' she claimed.

She added: 'We are not a Voodoo party, but we respect the spiritual aspirations of ordinary people and think this respect is the missing element in modern politics.'

Spirit is aiming for the much sought-after 'third party' in the U.S. – the vast army of non-voters, whose numbers are double those of either the Republicans or Democrats.

Meanwhile, day center custodian, Giorgio Jacopucci, was grumbling: 'I wish they'd told me to expect so many – we nearly had a riot.'

The old chain letters would say, 'A woman in Syracuse
refused to participate and her house burnt down: don't you refuse.'
Despite your grin, some fear would seep in. To disturb
Spirit's electorate, the next letters had some harmless herb
dust in the envelope corner; and the chain began as before,
spreading links outward, down Long Island's great curve,
spattering into the Bronx, and to the Birth of the Blues
in NY, that's Harlem; and meetings were staged as before.

This went along with scandalous irruptions
into official occasions, such as the famous interruption
of the Nuyorican festival one August in Central Park,
when Emen, Dolores, and a horde of Hispanic women, stark
naked, leapt on to the bandstand and invited all men
to strip the secrecy off their masculine pride and mark
the festival with a vow to end male domination
of politics, reviving an ancient spirit between men and women.

Will himself, poet of the poem, was still the first non-American
convert, a non-franchised alien, a BBC-speaking Scotsman
who'd seen a bit of the world. He told them all
at a party gathering in Brooklyn that he had a call
as a Bard to charter their progress: he had a scheme
– since occasional arrests and constant publicity put them on
Page Three so often – that he thought would appeal to more intellectual
audiences: and NYCU were planning a lecture. Thus went the scheme:

A great writer from Africa was warming on sherry in the wings,
a voice they admired, the hall packed, when Emen and her sisterlings
mounted to the mike. 'We're the Student's Party for Internal
Righteousness and International Tolerance,' she lied, but with a kernel
of truth, for it spelt SPIRIT. Because she was so black
no Uni official dared stop her: a photog from some journal
snap-snapped as Will joined her. 'Now listen to the things
this white man has written for those who aren't black.'

Will declaimed this:

WHITE CROSSROADS

'Ah'm to suck your asshole, stomp it,
ain't mah style. You tell it, baby,
you tell it, John, okay?
This is the play-off boy, you know it, I know it.'

All the propertied amusements, whether
Leona promised Trump to sell her lump
of land, or whether Wall Street crashes
only temporary within the lifetime
of the dispossessed, it's psychological poverty
of tired whites with lots of balls
pretending to speak for heterogeneous nations,
sadly moral faces of governors, wizened
with the humor of getting their own way.

Even if their millionaire bridges are breaking up
already thin smoke lines
of the new bridges arc above falling girders
and Catherine wheel firework tires
of phantom buses whisk across from City Hall.

'Ah'm to suck your asshole, stomp it,
ain't mah style. You tell it, baby,
you tell it, John, okay?
This is the play-off boy, you know it, I know it.'

At crossroads mental crossroads multiply
down by City Hall of Cities Going Wrong.
So white Manhattan manwoman white of sick tongue,
my white: my white shirtskirt, white of eyes,
newly arrived at crossroads of choice, as
white owner, leather attache box with locks,
moral owner manwoman me never could manage
Black bab bab voices crossing
smoked tarnish of tar of crossroads,
while Iyou white cross
to squash courts of whitened stainless steel,
fuckwords rising round us from legs
stretching out from walls. Me this
in other ways. Give up my plummy fucker voice.
Learn situation. Having left an English dream
half-finished, come abroad
seeking a voice change
to find that my voice must
crack open like a snake's egg for,
being its old self, whole and ineffectual,
it takes part in the real only by irony.

'Ah'm to suck your asshole, stomp it,
ain't mah style. You tell it, baby,
you fucking tell it, John, okay?
This is the play-off boy, you know it, I know it.'

My white life learns till middle age and stops.
Ask the white elderly what per cent
of their fellow world they've ignored.
Not too late in middle age to open out
to the Dahomey snakeloa, Damballah
the Voodoo-Santeria ordainer
whose red body wriggles along rainbows
whose venom spills yellow like egg purity,

the white skin of my life a container
of snaky kindship, moving in my moving limbs
across the crossroads, woman in me snaking,
my regard for myself priapic,
me, only a stranger, without right,
willingly drinking righteous venom
until white face becomes suddenly spotty,
along my lily forearm a white wart,
my eyes discoloring and seeing new colors,
vomit on the street like a yellow ochre city
seen from a satellite, not without beauty
in these Cities Going Wrong.
On a stoop a bar of soap, White barges Blacks,
a dropped neon tube explodes into argument.

'Ah'm to suck your asshole, stomp it,
ain't mah style. You tell it, baby,
you fucking tell it, John, okay?
This is the play-off boy, you know it, I know it.'

Voodoo's loa Attibon Legba
cannot rule my crossroads of white indecisions
but protects in my dreams the black crossroads
and protects thresholds of new lives
writhing with the principle of the snake.

Below Will the hall seemed a tray and the audience its sweetmeats
in ranks: their silence another of poetry's defeats.
But the African writer swirled out in her highly-hued dress
from the wings, beaming and gently applauding. Quite shameless,
the intellectuals awoke to clap. Alas the stewards were already onstage
and Will and Emen spent the night in jail. Their arrests
reached the *Post*, page 3, 'Caught clambering over the seats'.
Though Spirit, as party, was mounting, no one guessed the next stage.

For with first success came first danger. They got too busy,
forgot spirit, spent on stunts, mailings, had the hypocrisy
to trade on their 'Voodoo Party' label, in *Post* headlines
became 'The Hex', while Dolores fed the *News* other lines:
'Non-Voters Anon', 'The Stunt Pols', 'The Slaughtered Chickens',
'The Spellbound', 'The Underdogs'; and they always met deadlines,
until in the party inner circle Emen spoke out: 'We're the Non-Policy
Party with a party machine. That's not how the spirit quickens.

The students have printed Will's poem; it's drawn in some scholars,'
Emen said, 'bibliophiles of the asshole, linguists of the followers
of the dollar. But you see my eye bruise?' (Badly swollen temple.)
'I earned this recruiting in crack tenements: it's all too simple –
with middle class white faces now joining our variegated force,
and their Press seeking copy – to become some Aime Semple
Macpherson phenomenon and forget we're the party for non-voters.'
At that, the silent Cuban, High John, revealed his own force.

Spirit'd had no suspicions of High John, monosyllabic, statuesque,
once a bit battered, baggy in suits like the dispossessed
he seemed to be. Maybe if he'd been more flamboyant a bruiser,
a notorious heavyweight, not a quiet cruiser,
the members of Spirit, mostly women, would have pierced the pseudonym
given by Emen. Instead, they'd written him off as a loser.
Anyway he'd been absent three weeks. But now a sudden unrest
by the door revealed him, Conqueroo, fists high to suit his pseudonym.

He came from the shadows to show them he too had an eye bruise
and a swollen chin. 'I don't s'pose many you women read the *News*
sports page today,' he said with his usual grin. 'And none you scholars
did's for sure. But this here's a cheque for 3 million dollars,
'cos I'm the new light-heavy champ of the whole freaking world!'
Pandemonium, rustle, newspaper sharing, until the Cuban's gappy molars
stared out from the back page. 'You've never asked for my views,'
said High John, 'but I can help your non-voters to win over the world.'

'Don't make me scales of laughter in this room,' said Dolores.
'What we going to do with this money? You, boxer, it sure is
everything we fight against you bring here.' But the Cuban replied:
'Okay. Capitalism. My big fist. Thump, thump. Right,
I read you, Dolores. But I have a little Capitalist housing plan;
most it is for the inner circle. And allow me this: we hide
the 3 million from the media. Can't fight slam-bam if the story is
you fight for charity. And I take a few risks in my hidden plan.'

This plan led to tragedy later with the party under attack:
the inner circle of Spirit were involved not with the crack
dealers, said a Channel 9 special, but with *Behemoth*, the new Ecstasy.
Emen didn't waver, for she strongly admired the Cuban, and I...
that's the poet...Will...suspected...that is, he had suspicions...
well never mind...For love of Emen and of Spirit, he swallowed a lie
in her loyalty and, liking the plan, fell not far behind
in backing the Cuban, even when fighting the most public suspicions.

For the time we'll keep the plan hush-hush, but High John staged
strict auditions for some kind of play. Even Will plunged
those with his rendition of 'White Crossroads'. 'Good, but not enough
courage,' chuckled his wife. Yet though she might laugh,
a sadness invaded her during the secret rehearsals: the cast
seemed to play various ghosts, an old crone, a rough
Columbian with stereotype Uzi, cops, and some part the Cuban upstaged
them all with; he looked reckless, as if his die were cast.

One day there could be other Cities of Spirit, and the model
for action will constantly change; for now, we'll tell of the ritual
that first made the party famous. Emen asked Will for love to dress
her one night as she lay down. He placed a finger vertical to bless
the wet rind of her glistening pubis, so's to seal in the love,
locate the political in the personal and spiritual, her breasts kissed,
a pallid mood lifting, nipples caressed, a radical
pair of panties covered with hearts slipped up with his hands of love,

twin-heart sex shop strapless brassière, a dress golden
and red with more hearts, symbols of the loa of love in the olden
religion, the jet ringlets gleaming on her brown skull,
his male lips in the hairy perfume, the final kiss from Will,
and then she dressed him with the same care. That night,
he rose high on stage in his cowboy boots and told a thousand people
that they would now see someone lovely to behold in
his eyes, the mother-like, the loa-like, Erzulie that night.

'We are the gods,' Emen told them. It was her new thing. 'Who are
the gods? We, we, we are. We are in train–' (a rare
grammatical lapse in her oracular excitement) '– We are in train
of creating a ritual, yes a ritual for a politics beginning again
in the breath of spirit. There will be a tunnel, there will be a mirror:
we shall pass through; there will be an altar: we shall attain
mercy before it; there will be a book: we shall write our
deepest thought in that book, over a cross, glassy as a mirror.

The cross will be on a tomb – Christian enough for you Christians?
I'll be thinking of the Voodoo family Ghédé, and you Buddhist nations
can think of the great beyond; and you atheists can just shiver;
but one thing we'll all learn by the ever-flowing river:
you can't speak true politics unless you keep knowing you're dying.
We'll resolve conflicts, yes, but that creates others. I believe a
tremulous sense of the sacred, a goodness that frightens,
wins our hearts fully when a friend lies to rest by that river.

And that's how we'll create policy, and they will call us the gods,
the founders, the neglected people who against all odds
will bequeath their spirits to the future and become the loas.
Now, I know that only I and some others have Voodoo, that most
have no religion or have other dogmas; this is not the issue,
for our nature is half spirit and this must speak so as
to touch the deeply inter-communal in humans, the lightning rods
of sympathy which should flash in each political issue.'

For a moment she sobbed softly at the beauty of thoughts
none can share with another, Erzulie, loa, in her courts
of love, perfumed with flowers, coquettish in a dance,
spinning round, showing brown thighs, wooing the audience
to the spirit of love, poignant. 'D'you tell me of the homeless?'
she sighed. 'I tell you of homes in your soul, a residence
there for everyone: that's where we build first.
No creation of policy if it's our souls which are homeless.

We'll plunder religions for their best, make off with spoils
– deadliest ceremonies, altar paraphernalia, and sacred symbols –
we'll set up wide arenas, travelling temples made of wood
and canvas, rituals of the dead turning to good
in white tents enclosing night on darkening river meadows.
They'll be 'art shows' to the park authorities but we'll be understood
by people of spirit, meditating there until the mind fails
and the soul speaks of policy in the tents by river meadows.'

By F.D. Roosevelt Drive, bordering the ungentrified
Alphabet City of Avenues C and D, the Lower East Side
has its playing fields. New York's Parks Department,
told of a 'performance art work' (though 'art' meant
here the art of creating politics) left them alone.
Each non-voter would meditate in a tiny compartment
then pass through a tunnel to a tent, there, ritually, to decide
what Spirit should choose were it to have one policy alone.

And so the party referendum began. At first it seemed absurd.
Down by the river on grassy wasteland at dusk (the word
already spread by the correspondence network, funds upcoming
from the Cuban), flatbed trucks arrived amid a murmuring
crowd, a line of Portacabins went up, with a white tent central
and a wooden tunnel creakily winding towards it. Voodoo drumming
muffled on tambours. All on hire. Night fallen. Traffic heard
far-off. Otherwise silence. Non-voters in the cabins. The tent central.

Spirits sat down in darkness with their private mind,
these were party members squatting on stools behind
doors saying 'Occupied': they'd hired converted lavatories.
Lavatory, *hounfor*, cave, rushing water, wind through trees...
in isolation you can shed selfishness; shed
the pell-mell mind of self-interests until you find
your truest interest which you and others share. Rousseauist,
perhaps, but his citizens never squatted down in such a shed.

The faint urine smell was desirable; it anchored down
wandering thoughts; but as Mama Johnson for example hunkered down
in her shawl, on her stool, she, like all others, saw
a photo of cemetery crosses glimmering on the cabin wall,
and, like all others, heard a memory of voices in her head:
'Go be hard with men, chile, doan go be any more
hard with me, right? Liable pregnant her. Sank herself down
on ma sofa, stoned and risk of AIDS, just shit in her head.

'Shit, this place smellin of it. Did I tell you to watch the big guys
or what? I ain't talking to no Voodoo gods, but my eyes
shut all right, right? Praying into the heart of gold,
just like Emen told me, and I'm finding what? Old
Mr Pappy Man o' Mine, this heart finds you, this place
smells of piss. What's this? I see the urine trickling from cold
old bums in doorways, their blue black skin, slitty eyes
and damaged voices. My own old mama in that hospital place

'puffin at that oxygen tube, urinating in hospital, bare
black half moon ass, nurses wiping her drool, you doan care
'bout no politicky at the bed of death's for sure. Deep
things hover round her, come in your soul, doan quite weep
in your heart but get weepy for others' pain. I feel their power
in me now, working, that infected white baby next door, sleep
the last sleep, baby, with horrible blue black round your ear
spreadin' down your shoulders, I wan' you to take my power.'

Mama began a travail of spirit, the eyes of her own dead
mother looking at her. This poet leaves aside as sacred
her hatred of wrongs to her race, but all other hates
flicked mothy wings at her mother's blank stare, twin agates
which still saw *her*, and the moth wings departed.
Still, male street talk bothered her ears. 'Jessie states
this, Sharpton that...' but her dead mother's face shuddered
with underworld breath, and finally all street-smart departed.

'These death things in me working. Oh, we can't put none that
right, right? Not the death things. But death's what we got
for to purify life with. Now *that's* politics.
Good protestant me, none them juju tricks.
Just this soundless dagger of death stuck in my soul
and this piss leaking from old men's pricks,
old women's pussies, makes me feel alive. Thrilled. I've sat
long enough now. I'm clear, clear right to my daggered soul.'

A half hour in darkness. Mama Johnson lived close to suffering,
but other non-voters sat for hours, their culture buffering
them from such clarity: that politics begins with the knowledge of death,
at a moment of birth, a moment of marriage, mid-breath
in the death of minds, birth of minds, sharing of minds,
measure for measure. They sat until there was nothing left
in their thinking but the mid-moment, no false toughening
of attitude or wise cynicism, nothing but the sharing of minds.

A West-side lawyer came, scornful, and so spent two nights
encabined, wrestling with his demons, whereas three minutes
sufficed a Baptist minister, who opened his night's door and cried
'Hallelujah!' and so on, only to be mortified
when made to re-enter that darkness until he got kinder;
fast-thinking gays, closer than anyone to those who had died,
emerged weeping; and many failed and some started fights
when asked to retire; but those who voted had nearly all become kinder.

And we shall live in Ma Johnson's body, feel our stomach's weight,
breasts couched on it like elbows, troubled frown, heavy gait
swollen buttocks behind us under a print dress, an ache behind
our varicose knees as, feeling sombre, unusually kind
we climb out of our hut and tread damp, silvered grass to the tunnel,
where silently our people guard the entrance, a perfect mind
among us all, not our own. The wooden tunnel has a wooden gate;
the river gleaming across to Brooklyn; drumming in the tunnel.

Not yet a mass revival, this referendum, police car
flashing by the baseball diamond where a bonfire
lit the dancing, a line forming for the meditation,
a Haitian possessed by Ghédé – one form of elation,
the old East River in this spiritual, just a-rolling,
and Ma Johnson just a-strolling to the tunnel, proud in her nation
and in her body. 'I've got to keep my heaviness, my ugliness, entire:
that will light my fire, set the spirit rock and rolling.'

'Ouvway biyaay poor mwon,' was her password; they opened the wicket.
She mounted a ramp up to flat-bed trucks, set
at angles with others, bearing a 'tunnel' of rail wagon
bodies, gutted and linked together. Puffing, Ma Johnson
peered around in the close dark, smelt old food, but saw nothing
in the tunnel's first leg until a low lamp came on
in an alcove, where sat a fat black man, top-hatted,
a dead cigar in gap-teeth, bright smile full of nothing

except banquet: plump cummerbunded stomach, gold-
rimmed shades, lawyer-striped trousers, and old-
fashioned spats above spit and polish toe caps. 'Ouvway
biyaay?' Ma repeated hesitantly. No reply.
He sat on, cross-legged, obviously a party member
taking part in a fun house charade, with nothing to say
as the lamp went out, the floor creaked like ice, cold
futures ahead, warmth in the past she'd begun to remember.

In a present of many choices, a hand tapping her shoulder
made her spin round in the tunnel. A bright diorama
like a florist's window lit up to one side
a vista of real roses, but after a second they started to slide
sideways as stage machinery rumbled and were nudged out the way
by a panorama photo of graves. And who it was that had died –
whether her husband, her mother – she felt no one had told her,
and it would be herself one day, treading her graveyard way.

The short journey brought her to a final corridor
with a side table, two leathern chairs: an abandoned Pullman car,
a woman in white satin sitting there; she had a blue
stole, a sort of black Virgin Mary look, and she beckoned to
Ma Johnson to join her as she wolfed some wedding cake
beside a brass table lamp, her lips covered with goo
and her body breathing flower scents. Taking her place, Ma
nibbled, as directed, the sickly-sweet wedding cake

and found it falsely-happy opposite this wedded 'Mary'
who waited till she'd finished, then nodded, glanced away,
implying 'Now go'. (Unaware, Ma had passed an assessment:
anyone not solemn, any wrecker, anyone who offered harassment
in that car would by a trick of the doors be ushered
outside and calmed down by counselors. Ma Johnson's embarrassment
was acceptable.) She rose and walked on, remembering the day
of her own wedding but wrongly: she a burlesque bride ushered

along a deserted aisle to marry that woman,
call her Mary, Emen, Erzulie, someone not quite human
but large like her own soul. Down the corridor ahead
the exit now glimmered grey as all other lights cut dead
and walking towards the grey screen she saw an image
of herself approaching, waddling the way she had, a dead
spitting image in the same clothes, mimicking her every movement.
She passed straight through the screen, straight through her own image

as a curtain of silvered threads, that is, the 'screen', drifted
over her face and a whirring video camera clicked and stopped.
Suddenly fit for the occasion, Ma Johnson danced down a steep ramp
that led to a wide space of trampled grass, a damp
temple: overhead swooped shadowy wings of canvas
falling, skirting into walls; the dark air glistened, for an arc lamp
in the roof lit up a large mass on the ground, solid
wood that rose in black ledges; Spirit planned to canvass

political opinions on an altar. Now, this wasn't Voodoo
or the 'phenomenology of the transcendent self' – just a trick or two
for freshening up the normal, and Ma Johnson felt quite normal,
though she confronted a coffin sticking out of the altar: a funeral
despair and a hope of spiritual meaning transcending the religious.
The squared arches of many ledges formed a stepped mantle
over the coffin and each shelf bore icons, the Buddhas, the Hindu
figurines, a Koran, a minorah, a Toltec calendar, and not just religious

objects: a Humanist lapel badge, a philosophy book, 'The Sovereignty
of the Good' (for its title), activist posters, the rich plenty
of Civil Rights buttons. Above the coffin, dazzling on the altar,
lay a book whose pages were boldly handwritten. She felt a
fleck of water on her cheek as someone flashed out of the
shadows and sprinkled the grass with libations. They'd taught her
what to do next; so, whispering an oath to write down truth, and empty-
minded otherwise, she stepped forward, straddled the top of the

coffin and saw in its surface an embedded hologram: a white cross
seemingly swimming on blue waters, and at the criss-cross
was a hole like a mirror of waters, a depth we can sink
into, or from it dead souls may ascend if we think
of them as sunken. She moved till her knees were each side
of the cross now under her crotch in the darkness; she was a link
between upper and lower worlds; the book lay just across
from her on the ledge arching over the coffin, which from the side

formed the tongue of an altar-mouth, embedded with the hologram
on which Ma squatted. ('Must write. Rest my goddam mouth,'
she muttered. 'Momma up my middle. Or is it Jesus who is the Angel Mary?
Or my ancestors rising from some underwater island? Scary
feelings in my hand. Must write the three things Spirit must do.')
She wrote: 'I never wanted much, just goodness. I wish we'd been happy.
Oh but we can be!' ('Is that a thing? Okay then...') 'Make wealth,'
she wrote and added, 'for others, for the children, anything we do

has to help the future and make our dead mommas and daddies proud.'
('Is that two or three? Well...') 'Stop the garbage.' She spoke aloud
as she wrote: 'STOP ALL THIS GARBAGE, MA JOHNSON HAS SPOKEN...'
It seemed so trivial, yet she felt the whole world had awoken
as she looked at the book's instructions: 'Write the three
things that Spirit must do. Turn to a clean page in this book and
write the very first things in your mind. Don't be a coward
about this.' Now Ma had done so; and these were her three.

And *Newsday* made it all clear:

VOODOO PARTY CASTS SPELL
– OF AGREEMENT

Spirit, the political party rumored to act through Voodoo, claimed today that they'd found incredible agreement among the faithful about what party policy should be.

In a secret, two-month referendum, Spirit set up a funhouse on meadows bordering New York's East River.

At night, party members meditated in cabins, then walked through bizarre tunnels before entering a tent arranged like a temple. There, they straddled a coffin, and in a book resting on an altar wrote down their recommendations for policy.

'Call it supernatural or what, of the 1,000 members we had time to ask, 98% came up with an identical policy program,' said Spirit spokesperson Will Penniless.

'It's amazing. Once everyone's in the right frame of mind, we all know what a political program should look like.'

This was the program:

- Make material wealth for other people, spiritual wealth for ourselves. (Some, mostly men, specified that 'other people' meant the 'third world' or the 'homeless'. Some, mostly women, specified, 'Help our neighborhood first.')
- The only qualification for party membership should be goodness and respect for the history and future of the people's individual families.

- Long-term earth environment issues must have first consideration to save resources that our children's children should inherit.

Mr Penniless said this meant: 'Evidently not an end to the making of wealth. We can't help anyone without listening to the business lobby.'

The point was to make greed go out of style, so that more desirable ways of using wealth result and that individual fortunes should not be amassed.

'Following one suggestion, we shall hand out year's suspensions – in a kindly way – to members who use normal political manoeuvres to destroy party happiness and decency.'

As for environmental issues, Spirit wants to confront popular opinion by cutting down on private car use, domestic trash and industrial waste. One voter just wrote: 'Stop this garbage.'

What about drugs and crime, and, if there's less of hydrocarbon pollution, unemployment? Policing, rehabs, housing, international relations even - no real change in practical policies can come until the moral climate has changed, the party claims.

The Era of Dispute began. Marxists and anarchists, observing
the rise of the party, infiltrated meetings, noisily swerving
every debate into a grab for power. 'Power! Power!' –
'Pyuuhh! Pyuuhh!' Emen would reply, pointing a pistol finger.
Church persons, too, sought to color all talk with their god. Spirit
politely asked some of these serpents to retire for a year:
then the slithery could come back on their own feet, deserving
to pass through the gate if they'd open their doctrines to Spirit.

Some non-voting students joined up and the agency newsman Peter Belia
(or 'Belly Belia', pronounced 'Memorabilia'),
brilliant, Blakeian, Zoa-like, jowls full of politics, T-shirt
of bottlegreen vinyl formed as if from leaves, pert
eyes with arched brows meeting in hooks. Leftist clichés
dazzled like coins on his lips: ozone, brokers hitting paydirt,
greenhouse effect, endangered forests, Nicaragony, Cubaphilia,
constitutional change, freeze on Wall Street dealings...But the clichés

made more than one eye gleam, for the great belly had swallowed
up Pentagon strengths on this missile, what House rules allowed,
who was deputy foreign minister in Burkina Faso – the Belly
had met him – who were Haiti's more notorious torturers, naturally
he'd met them, which made Emen shudder; above all he was expert in
the failure of American third parties, being himself a revolutionary
totalitarian who believed in the schizoid as authentic: few followed
him there, but some were impressed by all he was expert in.

He fell in the purges for decency, which gilded the party with fame
for the first time, as the Voodoo label dropped limply off and the name
became simply: pure Spirit. Belia and his kind were a venomous
enemy if we're still talking Paradise. A second enemy was
an influx of white liberalism, of those whose own nation
did not live under day-to-day threat, and even your poet must
repeat that he lacks right to speak, yet must speak all the same
in honor of what he is not, of all that Baraka calls 'nation'.

For decency may also be dangerous: it opens the door for the brutal;
and while the deprived rage, it's there smiling, utterly futile
in its wish to be liked, to do right, to avoid discord, unease.
Yes, it rots the union of races it seeks; it's often a social disease
because it can't tolerate strangeness and mystery in others and secretly
it, too, seeks for power: as if the unengaged self, wishing to please
everyone, might also dominate them. Yes, nothing more subtle
than this enemy, which could survive these purges – but secretly –

– but secretly.' The line's lame. The plot simultaneously sticks.
A poem gets stuck at a point; you can find it; the music is
always faulty there. Step back in the dance of the verse
and you see that the thought had already flagged, or, worse,
couldn't solve its problems. We were warned of this from the start:
'No one penniless can found a political party'; the poem stutters
to a halt at that point; the party not fully political, the public's
attention not fully caught. Go back; find the music; restart.

The music begins in each point over again, the beats that unite
the flow of melody into infinitesimal perceptions. And within each beat
the overall form is anticipated; so the past is caught up in the present:
the future breathes in the point. Here is the clue to the decent
founding of politics in a poem: that the future comes alive
now: that the neighborhood is to the world as the moment
is to the whole; unlike the politicos, poets get their world right
if the point and the flow of the whole are united in beats: all alive

now and thrilling with the future. And so I look for the singer
who will sing the next part of the song truly. And I find her
making love: any woman. 'Our world,' she dreams, 'is shining with promise,'
and she spreads her labia for the pearled and purpling head of the penis,
while the man thinks: 'Point, point, penetrate right to the source
of time,' and she: 'Keep it moist with promise, for this
is our whole world weeping with joy, a gaseous planet, a voyager
through the ethereal to time's borders, pulsing out from the source.'

PART 2

Yuhwa Lee, Lee Yuhwa also, in Queens, at 4 a.m.,
or are you one of the thousand Kims? So different from Emen
but now our standard-bearer, engaged in the same sexual act
as she, you on top: your husband, Juan, Hispanic. Only through mixed
marriage of minds can Spirit come into full being,
for Korean-Chinese-Japanese stand apart, wanting only an intact
economy in which to practice their aggressive capitalism.
Not to be racist, Spirit must be full, 'full' being

difficult to describe, when the stores run by other people
are threatened by square-shouldered Korean work ethics. Yuhwa Lee
had tossed aside a students' weekly from Seoul: its 'wits'
had written: 'Oh, EHWA Women's University recruits
male students: I may take the admissions exam. Better choose
the Home Economics. After graduation...perhaps it's
a man I should marry' – to Yuhwa, this reminiscent of Seoul,
its sexism still alive in her new community, much as she'd choose

her own people above others. But Juan, one of the new Hispanics,
had joined with her in reformed sexual politics,
and now wanted her to join Spirit. She with her bright
Republican mind: in its darkness an electrically lit
honeycomb, an America of rooms, each clean as a Korean restaurant:
inside each room, a neat capitalism, orders in place, no get-out
from unceasing hard work, a Confucian familism, business
ethics that begin in a Christian church or a Korean restaurant.

She and Juan were joking, with tags from that magazine,
as they gyrated on the bed: on top, she felt obscene
in a nice way. 'Oh, I am hurting for money,' she said with feeling,
feeling quite different really. Juan sighed at the ceiling,
'How about practising the alcohol reaction?' 'No more thought
of drinking,' she trilled scornfully. 'Let's play at see-sawing.'
He picked up on the script: 'The top person is like a stock concern
whose 60% profit left investors bankrupted.' 'No more thought,'

she grunted, 'let's do away with such a non-productive math.'
And pinching his glans, she disclosed the slit, one path
to the human unity of number, then furtively, like shop-lifting,
stuffed it under her, settling back, buttocks uplifting
and down-posing, while she still talked, chirpy as a bird in Korean
sing-song. 'Yankee politics–it lost its way, Europe shifting
all its power balances, East no longer enemy so much, don't laugh
when I'm UP talking please: I'm being DOWN to earth, very Korean.

'Yankee politics brain-dead,' said Representative Obey, *Times* today.
No one can make speeches no more: consultants tell them: 'Okay
sentiments but too *risky* for say in public.' 'Got
question for you, Pol, what kind of 30-second spot
they going to make TV out of that?' asks consultant.
No debate left in Congress. Three election issues: What
money in bank? Who your media adviser? Can they take away
your mustache? It's con, con, con, con-sultant

all the way.' With mustacheoed dreamy smile, Juan came beneath
her in political unity and rhythm. She grimaced through her teeth
and continued: 'No wonder your people lose all respect. Respect
me, I respect you. Simple. Crawl to me, give me money, then expect
me to think you slime. A cynical people, a cynical no-showvote.
Listen, in Seoul we got terrible politicos, graft, spies, select
your opponents, rough 'em up. And still we got some kinda belief
in government. Everyone's gotto vote, vote, vote

or there's no aaah!, life.' Her turn. She rose in dignity
like a mare rising. Her bedroom displayed a Christian civility:
wall photo of Seoul, its mountains topped with huge TV mast
surrounding the plunge of white skyscrapers, all the past
her family had lived. Her ink-stones in obsidian, white
writing-brushes, wood lanterns, kiss curls on pink-faced
figurines: yellow and red panels, thick calligraphy: in a pretty
picture, Jesus, Korean speech balloon but he Jewish-White.

'Thing is, you can't draw the liver out of a flea,' she said,
dressing. 'I join your party I gotto organize some trade
for you, small business lines, we Koreans know well. Now don't
get worried, no grasping capitalism, we work for party. I won't
do no thing your Emen don't agree. But you can make each neighborhood
finance center for Spirit. You come along with me to Hunt's Point
market, right now Juan, I show you how to make a bed
of roses out of fresh produce, a Spirit shop in our neighborhood.'

As cabbage leaves drift on the sidewalk, and cherries, squashed, bleep
their stones, ice sparkles under broccoli, the washed beans seep
water through slats of wood out at Hunt's Point, and it's only 6.30,
the wholesale market already almost done, the rest of the city
barely waking as the dawn gleams on unsold boxes of onions,
the trucks in circles like cowboy wagons, the gutter clogged with dirty
produce – a cab draws up from Woodside. Juan and Yuhwa step
out, staring at these early risers who return, squeeze the onions,

in case they've missed a dollar. And beauty curls its lip, and Spirit
turns away. For this is trade, whose only merit
in poetry is to fund sentiment and bourgeois drama and treacle
family life, steady ascensions above poverty; trade's vehicle
like a heavenly car, bears the business soul up to the clouds
of international enterprise. Juan, like Will a poet, had little
taste for buying and selling. While Yuhwa, lithe as a ferret,
slipped from stall to stall, his head was lost in clouds

of romance: revive neighborhoods, yes, but day to day labor,
no romance there. His eye caught suddenly a Korean neighbor
from Woodside, a grandfather, squatting by the kerb, in his palm
a translucent plastic box, misting, as he packed in farm
raspberries for the store, the compound-eyed seeding of the fruit
weeping and the speckled crimson cushions kept from harm
in his cupped hand, a careful installation, like a favor
paid, a nestling in richness as plastic closed over fruit.

Juan knelt. 'May I buy that?' he said. 'Here's 10 dollars' –
so badly he wanted it. Box and money changed hands, the oldster's
eyes black anemone blobs under grey hair waves.
At four or so, the child plays with money purchase, saves
real cash at five; so, in civilization's childhood, money
comes in early and is not ugly: someone craves
the beauty of the fruit, a way is found that answers
that need: the berries glow: the dullness is just money,

and represents absence. When humans exalt this absence into holiness,
not 'value' but 'profit, price, trade', then ugliness
begins its necessary rule…Well, Yuhwa got a loan
in a Woodside basement, another member of her Korean
church rotating the credit that had got him started; and a store
was bought in Morrisania. 'See?' she said, 'For Emen
and Spirit to take over one day. D'you think Her Holiness'
Emen (this, jealousy) will bow down and consider our store?'

Now celebrated, the project, 'Buying back the Neighborhood'
dates from this time, though Dolores and her sisterhood
objected at Yuhwa's Opening Feast. 'Having fun? Look, we have Af-Am
and Hispanic peoples, the Caribbeans, a few whites, not many Jews – am
I just racist if I ask what of Chinese and Koreans? Don't they stand
apart? Will Spirit just switch on, switch off, if the Asian
communities aren't with us? Getta a capitalist, getta hood,
lissenan where do we stop? Or, rather, where do we stand?'

In Morrisania? Your store in my neighborhood, where I radicalize
the people? Dirt money from Seoul's going to open our little Bronx eyes?
Huh!' A speedy-gay, lawyer-rasp voice broke in – Lou Levinson –
joined up with the journalist Peter Belia but stayed – 'Listen
to the Korean, Dolores: afterwards radicalize. I gave my youth
to law – hundreds of corporate paydirt deals and then some.
We've got multi-national input here: with all you guys
we'll turn Capitalism about-face, give Morrisania back its youth.'

Dolores spat back: 'Hear of one Ramon Rueda, with his Mao Ze-dong
cap, an' his People's Development gangers? Squatted a Washington
Ave block, Bronx, in the 70s, homesteaded it with city loans,
made it a showplace. In came a President to Carterize Ramon's
dreams of a model village for the poor, Ramon's pay rising
to 30 grand as he hit stardom. Then came the fights and arson's
charred visit to PDC offices. Ramon disappeared, all the ranting
finally amounting to little. Ha! Morrisania not rising.'

Emen eased her breasts on the table top: 'Dolores, you left-wing, honey,
me Haitian, Juan from Puerto Rico, Yuhwa with her money
from Seoul, Will with his WASPISH *paw-try*, Mr High John,
Cuban capitalist *de la quint' essence* – cash from K.O.s – and Ma Johnson,
with her Harlem wisdom, are talking true together: aim to join us?
You and Lou Levinson? While we buy up this whole section our intention
can't be public, has to be *petit-à-petit*, act a little funny,
be a little dense, and house to house get residents to join us.'

High John had arrived in a chauffeured Merc: he was taking an airing
before the next day's championship bout. His trainer, despairing,
skulked behind smoked glass and the boxer had entered, tired,
perhaps of training: his politics were suspect but most admired
his generosity though Emen worried that he lacked center. 'Soon enough
Dolores,' he said, 'a little drama in your *barrio*. Look, I haven't retired
yet: 'nother win tomorrow, with my purse and a little bit daring,
'*Vinceremo!*' iffn I get that money working fast enough.'

Some sat round the long table, some round the noodle table with its side
dishes of baked, raw and broiled meats, fried
vegetables, kimchi, soup. 'Korean cookery's a marriage
of two dominating ideas, say China and Japan, having the courage
to make a third new thing, leaner, fitter for the nation,' orated Will.
Long table: rice, bun soup, raw fish, more kimchi. 'Not to disparage,
the Korean,' he added. 'Now New York's like a nation, whose died-
in-the-dish politics has lacked *cuisine*: watch and we'll

put new ingredients in the recipe,' Will said. 'The wealthier Japanese
let's set aside – and the up-town Chinese, but we need a down-town Chinese
member.' They found a waiter, Peter Sung, and added one of the calmer
homeless people who hung around their meetings, Georg, a peasant farmer
from Mittle Europe who'd hit the bottle in New York, but had a lifetime
knowledge of greens. Then Peter pierced through their radical armor:
'All profits ploughed back, all work at very low pay. You get happiness,
if you your own boss. No unions. Experience of lifetime.'

Members of Spirit honored the Wobblies and the early heroical
unions; like them, this poem is scandalized at Peter's unradical
approach to wages. Pay low pay! A squabble broke out
between Dolores on the Marxist edge and Koreans standing out
for family advancement. But Peter just said, 'Low pay
means good life. Capitalism powerless. See? All talk about
greed, waste, environment – all depend on paying people
more than real need. S'great, S'great on low pay

providing you pay yourselves.' An over-heated Dolores,
(husband dead, you gossip mongers), who had rather liberal mores,
took Peter to bed that night. She blinked telephone switchboard eyes
at his thin ribs, his penis grey-wigged, at the peasant-wise
face-lines taking her round and round many smiles. He, half
his life womanless ('a Kwang Tung ancient, a historical prize,'
Dolores was thinking), experimentally poked her thick forest
and cupped her curdling buttocks, dividing them gently in half.

Dolores, her mind boiling with argument, enflamed by Puertorriqueno
radical rhetoric, now divided herself; she opened the 'O'
at the center of mood. To describe aging lovers at work
seems intrusion. But we forget Legba and the unvarying fork
upon fork of his crossroads. Two paths cross. The center is sucked
down and up into the divine. At a liquid point, at a rhythmic jerk
of a naked penis, Dolores formed her full lips into an 'Oh!'
full of good humor and spitty remarks; then she set to and sucked,

and this was the idea she sucked in: though Peter's orgasm was feeble
(low pay), Spirit grew warm between them, a church without steeple.
Low pay had divided her right and her left thigh. Marxism:
give us high high pay, the workers' just share. Capitalism:
give them high pay to a point, for exports are built on home
sales, and the cash coming in from abroad is the jissom
that signals the standard of living has risen all round. An inescapable
logic either way. 'But what if we took less pay home?'

wondered that dyed-in-the-wool radical, Dolores. Home sales
would fall, but if we didn't *mind* that, made ourselves
Third World workers almost, exporting generously from the self outward,
the bigshots would be delighted at first: competitiveness restored!
More pay for them! Exports would increase, the bosses get richer
while unions howl; and then one day a nation restored
would cry, 'Enough!' Low pay has brought back our spirit; the scales
shall be balanced: we simply take the wealth of those who got richer

while we were learning the lessons of spirit and use it for national
purpose, limiting personal wealth by a ceiling, the only rational
polity. (By extension of logic, the spread of cheap exports would cut
world demand, lessen Third World tensions, tend to even out
international incomes, and do wonders for the environment.)
Pure idealism, of course, But this is a poem; and it's not
not going to happen. Readers may try but can't become cynical:
the poem has decreed the penniless will win: it's a closed environment.

The story of Spirit and the drug, Behemoth (it made you walk tall,
the biggest beast in the world – citizens kept to the wall
when anyone BM'd walked by)... that story of Bad Mind
has its place here, as the party set out to refind
Spirit in Morrisania section, the Bronx. Secret rehearsals
have earlier been mentioned, as if a drama were being refined
for public performance. If so, it concerned drugs, property, real
dangers run by the actors, and death foreshadowed even in rehearsals.

The Cuban, through a front company, bought a condo infested with rats
and Behemoth dealers: 'Dirt cheap,' he grinned. 'It's the dirt that's
costing the money.' His next fight, well he bought him another.
Condo A he refurbished – not too much – every brother
and sister of Spirit gave their labor, their civic virtue,
as they would in this Bronx, Dolores's section. However,
condo B: he let the druggies in. Lawful families from B found welcome mats
when they moved out to A, a comfy haven of civic virtue.

Each apartment in B had roaches, sure, but microphone bugs
in the walls too; the wiring ran down to the basement where, under rugs,
an ancient Hispanic lady, Madre Hubbard, kept miniature recorders
sunk below floorboards. Madre Hubbard was really Dolores
in disguise, acting as spy, willing to stash Behemoth
for short spells if the guys on her stoop gave the orders.
The Cuban kept the attic. He was absentee, covert, one of the cogs
in high-level dealing. In his attic he also stored Behemoth.

The Fat Men, the major Columbians, thought they'd the mystery man
over a barrel. On the take but careless, in possession
of the stash, he'd get landed out front if a crash came,
while they'd disappear. Strangely, right then, in the fight game
High John reached his peak, fighting almost for joy,
feeding off risk, conscious of purpose, a boxing Hall of Fame
slot secure; but the joy secret – that the druggy population
who bought the Behemoth would only enjoy

its heady delights for a moment; and some were members of Spirit,
their funds recycled for use in false buying. A demerit
of the scheme (low pay) was depletion of High John's income;
but he didn't mind. In an intimate moment he told Emen
how he'd lost a brother to Behemoth, after dabbling himself, a debt
he now was repaying. The main thing he worried
about was that real addicts bought from the dealers. 'When we come
to defeat this evil,' he said, 'I can never repay *that* debt.'

Oh cynical New York, everyone so smart: riots, marches answering
corruption and bad government. Citizens cynical or despairing
cause this: constantly blaming party machines that are voted
for. It only needs a burying of precise platform, voters devoted
to the one end: their city and its cleanliness of heart. An end,
then, to that pride of the breakfast table or the street corner, the toted
solutions with scornful citation of newspaper stories, everything
smart-answered, the means questioned, questioned without end.

Oh New York, remember the Cuban and Dolores who suffered! Simultaneously
five schemes were put into action: the Drug Bust, the Drug Rehab, the
Bank Scam, the Store Score, and the Yuppie Cream. When the Behemoth
dealers and users filled every apartment in Block B, sloth
and crazed violence marked its corridors and environs. Block A
now had a ground level store, run by Yuhwa and some tough
Spirit Party members, working to Korean discipline; and gradually
the neighbors shopped there only, in the store called 'Block A'.

Store profits siphoned up to the attic of B, to the 'unknown' owner;
rumor said he was running an illicit bank and that a loaner
could get top interest, plus laundering of any soiled dollars.
The attic door was of steel, with a grille, and Peter Sung's molars
greeted the callers: even the drug lords did their 'laundry'
there. Yet no one saw cash leave the building. (A lift on oiled rollers
ran down the old chimney to Dolores – Madre Hubbard – that 'loner'
in the basement, and she took it out.) Not trusting so sudsy a 'laundry',

the drug lords mounted a guard. One dawn, old Mo
Hubbard bundled off with her bags, unremarked. Later, a limo
with smoked windows drew up close and the drug guards thought
that Peter had climbed in as the car drove off – at least, they'd caught
a glimpse, but a crowd of women apparently gossiping had obscured
Peter's escape back through a basement window; so the guards bought
the feint; and their bosses, over the walkie-talkies said, 'Follow
that car', and it went, empty, back to its garage, which obscured

the trail. The guard's remnant rushed upstairs to the steel door,
now labeled: 'This bank has failed and was outside the law.'
(Legitimate debtors got their bills in the mail.) Cars
raced off to the front company's offices. Shut. The drug czars
couldn't believe the nerve of this classic bucket shop act
and started detective work, you'd better believe, in the bars
and stores of the neighborhood. That same day, all the poor
users and rich dealers in B, got a message, 'Clean up your act

and your neighbors will help. If not, get out.' But who was the landlord?
They looked out the window: the building was surrounded by a silent horde
of women, five deep in a circle. They were besieged. Now the police
appeared, drawn by the crowd, and it became a national news piece:
the women who wouldn't allow drugs in or out, although food
was sent in. After two days, the desperate users gave up in peace,
leaving the dealers inside, unable to shoot, starved
now, abandoned by their bosses, surrendering at last for food.

Newsday reported Day 1 like this:

WALL OF WOMEN FOILS DRUG SHOOTOUT

An iron wall of women, five deep, encircled a tenement block and foiled a drug-related shootout in Morrisania yesterday, after a sting operation by persons unknown ripped off hundreds of thousands of dollars from Behemoth gangster Bigs.

Police were called to the tenement at 778 Miramont when the silent women assembled for no apparent reason about 8 a.m.

It turned out that an illegal bank plus a Behemoth supply depot had been established in the penthouse. Drug lords, wooed by high interest rates and profit laundering, had cautiously lent the 'bank' money, thinking their own fire power would deter any sting by the bank's proprietors.

While they took quick advantage of the interest rates, they mounted a guard across the street to make sure banked money was not whistled away from the building which is full of Behemoth addicts and dealers.

But by an elevator concealed in an old chimney route down the walls, both drugs and money had been conveyed down to a ground-floor apartment. At dawn yesterday, Sting Day, the ground floor tenant, Madre Hubbard, a 75-year-old Hispanic, escaped with the loot past the drug guards' eyes. She is still on the run.

Behemoth Bigs figured that the concealed elevator meant involvement of the tenement's owners, Part Meant Estates, and planned a mid-morning raid on the company's Spring Street offices. Another slap in the face awaited them: the company had done a moonlight flit, leaving the Bigs hundreds of thousands of dollars out of pocket.

Back at the tenement block, the gangster guard got walkie talkie orders to invade the building. As two of the armed guards crossed the street, they ran against a wall of women confident that they couldn't use their guns.

While the gangsters dithered, the police arrived, and the gunmen fled.

So far no one knows:

- Who owns the tenement
- Who really lived in the penthouse
- Who was the Chinese man who acted as bank teller
- Where Madre Hubbard has gone with the cash and drugs

Red-faced drug lords have gangster-detectives combing the streets, competing with police to find the answers.

Today the women are still besieging the building, trying to force the dealers and addicts to leave by refusing to let food or drugs in or out. One woman said: 'Everything's on the grapevine, so no one can get picked off as a leader or for knowing too much or anything.'

She added: 'There's a new feeling in this neighborhood. That's what we're responding to.'

Police spokesman, Lt. George Keeley, says: 'We'll leave this siege in place. It's a force for peace and without it who knows what would happen?'

They'd smoked out Behemoth by Day 30. (Taped evidence
of major supply lines had been handed on to the cops, but since
that's not a Spirit story, we'll leave it.) Building B
became a co-op – not a yuppie paradise, of course, with enormously
inflated values, but something more modest: nevertheless, a profit
was made, and then with two buildings renovated and a lot of money
both licit and illicit freed for further buying, a new confidence
trick was played upon capitalist forces, creating yet more profit.

Property C was bought. Now the party store run by Yuhwa and Juan
with neighborhood help was booming; it had leaked out to everyone
that profits for Spirit bought buildings: almost a boycott operated
on shops which lacked party blessing – not that they intimidated
customers: it was just the buyers' choice. They sold the store
at its peak of success to a capitalist chain, which over-rated
its prospects, since the contract banned Spirit from opening another one
in competition. But because the capitalists set all their store

by contracts, they under-rated neighborhood networks. Extra-legally
a store promptly opened in the third property, C, and all the
customers transferred. This shop was owned by a consortium of residents
(using secret 'laundry bank' funds). The first store slumped and the incensed
capitalists were without comeback: no law had been broken, except that
the neighborhood gave its profits to Spirit, just as presidents
of capitalist corporations support the Republicans. Property C
rose in value and the party was gaining in power, except that

protection was given to *all* local firms, many of whom paid
dues to the party willingly. So it went on: mutual aid
for renovation, in the fight against drugs, all increase in value
kept in the residents' control, some co-ops, gradually new
small shops receiving neighborhood loyalty: we may leave
the detail: the struggle bitter, violence rife – soon a few
Italians and Irish lent aid. A financial basis was laid.
Order advances, neighbor helps neighbor, and criminals leave.

Meanwhile, in Manhattan, a meaty bone had been left beside
that sleeping dog, the City Council – in fact, more a great side
of beef. The Estimates Board had been dissolved; the Mayor,
seeking budget approval, had to go to a council become bull-terrier.
In a bad move for the party machines, they'd added a third
more Council districts – and Spirit, pointing like a lurcher
at the scent, now realized that ethnic minorities had
failed to increase their members on Council by that third.

Of the 51 seats in the next poll, Spirit candidates mopped up
20, giving them the sway of the balance and the invite to sup
with a long spoon at the devil's banquets of politics. Patronage
from the pols was refused. Came news from an upstate village
that a Spirit party had formed, then in LA, and Seattle awoke,
and Washington realized at last that this was part of the slippage
of Congress from voter affection: Spirit, a jester, had its lip
at the cup of power: the FBI turned an eye as Washington awoke.

Morrisania, a play within the play of Spirit's success,
now reached its tragic denouement. Remember Peter Belia, the memorious
journalist, who was ousted during the Decency Purge? He'd saved
his revenge for two TV one-shots. The first asked, 'Is Spirit depraved?'
and revived the old 'Voodoo Party' label. A headless goat,
the remains of a sheep, sundry chickens, and a white dove had
been found in a New Jersey rail siding. 'Obviously a Spirit sacrifice,'
claimed Mr Belia, thinking privately, 'This'll get Emen's goat.'

'Pamphlets from Spirit were found in a nearby boxcar,' he intoned.
'Does Spirit only gain power from magic and blood? Stay tuned
for reactions from Christians Fighting Satanic Crime – after this break.'
The fade-out paused on the wretched goat. Belia and his fake
outrage returned to the screen with a really damaging charge.
'Spirit pretends to be radical. Where's its support from the Black
activists?' Appearing beside him, a virulent Marxist, a little stoned,
accused Emen of appeasement, of pacifism, of abandoning her charge.

Belia's Shot Two, 'compiled with the help of anonymous sources',
exposed High John the boxer as the laundry bank banker and Dolores as
Madre Hubbard. Belia re-ran the clips of their cash heist,
showed how the ring of women stopped them all getting iced,
and asked, 'Where's that money now?' (His sources were criminal,
and they wanted to know too.) 'Was this High John's highest
paid fight, a fight against drugs, to add to his boxing resources?'
Belia asked. 'What's the difference between this hero and a criminal?'

Even today, Emen wears on her breast a pendant of jet,
for Belia caught them in an impasse and she kept silent. The profit
had gone to the store scam, and High John refused to clear
his name by endangering the party. 'I'll get on with my fightin' career,'
he said. 'No one's goin' to touch the champ: don't get soft:
the cops loved us!' The night of a title defence drew near
and High John became strangely withdrawn as he trained. He kept fit
but the snap went out of his sparring; he was the one going soft.

Making a thin trail through a stormy forest, the champ and his team
entered the stadium that night, a tangle of arms, a victorious beam
in High John's eyes as he wrassled through his fans. Distant trumpet
fanfares came far off in the forest from some mountain parapet
out of sight in this dark and furious tunnel; and the blue ring
the red ropes and brilliant lights drew them on. A shot. A bullet
blasted the boxer's forehead wide open. A frightening scream
from elsewhere. The boxer slumped in the aisle and lay shuddering.

The gunman escaped in the melée; the fighter was stilling in death;
and the stadium quietened, shocked: open mouths, held breath.
And again the frightening scream pierced the silence. Oh, it was Dolores
at ringside, her hands to her ruined eyes. As deep in that forest
the boxer had fallen from the assassin's bullet, a flask of vitriol
had been hurled into Dolores's face. There was an arrest...
two little crowds within the vast fight crowd...but let us leave
in sorrow this boxer dying and Dolores scarred by vitriol.

PART 3

The boxing world, bitter against Spirit for 'ruining a fighter's career'
('sport comes first'), grabbed on to the funeral. They draped the bier
in blue satins surmounted with vermillion gloves and hired seven black
horses with pompoms. In the coffin, of ebony shellac,
High John lay low in his ring strip. Past and present champions
headed the cortege, TV cameras were high in apartments, a crack
brass band started up...but then other crowds began to appear
along the route – whole neighborhoods – to honor a different champion

from that of the fight fans: not just Morrisanians, but any in New York
who could give their hearts to a martyr; they flocked to the sidewalk
as High John passed by, and boxing made way for the real world.
The sober air grew full of cheering, Spirit's flags unfurled
over thousands of heads, the procession swelled with High John's joy.
From Madison Square Gardens it turned down Sixth Avenue, whirled
into Fifth, Emen at the head, the promoters engulfed. A cork
had flown from bottled up sentiment; and the people released their joy.

Mid-town, a motorcade took over the burden, sweeping out of Manhattan,
the boxing 'fraternity' escaping with the dead hero draped in his satin.
Their route lay to Queens, graveyard of New York, but Spirit members
jumped into yellow cabs and followed, over East River, under the girders
of the Williamsburg Bridge, and down to the cemetery, where this was the scene:
two TV vans, a fanfare of trumpets as if from the ring, 'Boxers remember
The Champ' on a banner, cabs screaming up – and a strange pattern
of rainbow-robed people, squatting by graves, some distance from the scene.

Feet first, High John had traveled to these smart suburbs of Queens,
feet first to the blinding white tombs and the lawn-smooth greens
of the cemetery, the fight crowd muscling in, walling round
the grave, blocking out Spirit, hogging publicity for the pound-
for-pound best fighter of his era, protecting that last ditch
and its false glory. A promoter began a round-by-round
summary of a 'great career' (oh, fights ennoble, ordinariness demeans
'the Hero'). But a fat little man, who was making a last ditch

attempt to get in on the action, came wiggling through. Black activist,
Islamic preacher, a Holy Book held high in his fist
(High John had been no believer), knowing he could rely on
everyone else's decorum, he began his familiar oration:
poverty caused crime; white racism caused poverty in the Black
or Hispanic sections. 'Has no one caught the real lesson
of High John's war against drugs?' he bellowed. 'Each white racist
has created these hoods – I mean neighborhoods *and* Columbian or Black

gangsters –' The boxers were ready to punch him out, but a veiled
woman in black appeared in their midst, a dumpy person, who railed
at the 'preacher': 'D'you suppose Spirit doesn't believe anythin'
you can say about racism? You got divine truth or somepin'?'
(Of course, this was Dolores and she was half-weeping.) 'You dare face
me and tell me what you done, 'cept shout your goddam fuckin'
mouth off? We go buying back a whole hood, High John bailed
us out for the cash, ok fuckin' activist, tell me to my face

what you done?' Dolores whipped off her veil. Her face was grained
like wood by the vitriol, scars and tributaries, eye corners stained,
skin flat-planed, roughened, a whorl, and a little knotted stuff,
the voice, once shrill and perky, now basso, turned a little gruff.
'I gotta letter here, you flaky big boxing promoters in your sable fur
collared overcoats, says, 'Hi, from High John.' This is enough
to shut you boxers up for ever.' Her eye-corners rained
down tears as she took out the letter. 'What d'you think he fought for,

you money junkies? Listen: 'Hi, from High John. They're gonna get me,
sure. And I'll have a burial, sure. You'll all forget me,
sure – a line in the fight encyclopedias, maybe. Well, it's my funeral,
so here's what. I started out fighting the world, while that mortal
brother of mine began his fight with the needle. Well I won
and he lost. Emen changed all that – pardon me Will,
for I admire meekness and she will always be yours – but let me
place my murder at the party's *service*, till we've won

each goddam election we're boxing for. And shaddap, you tight
ass boxers at my burial. Only one thing I want. All you, unite,
left-wing African-Americans, Spirit, the good whites, Koreans,
Muslims, Rastas, Peter Sung and his Chinese, you all discuss what it means
to have spirit, there, right by my graveside, so I can lie upwards
and stare at you above, smile on my face. Dolores, queen of queens,
you tell them in Queens that High John's fighting his last fight
on his back, dead and full of Spirit, his Spirit rising upwards."

Like a crane grab, Dolores sprang down and straddled the coffin, her feet
braced against earth. The afternoon light fell dead-beat
on her damaged face; and it was a witch-doctor's mask with dark
eye sockets and cheeks decorated by strips of whitened bark.
She squatted over High John as if his soul could pass into
her crotch – Ma Johnson had squatted like that once, though the shellac
here had no cross hologram, just an invisible, dead heart
below. And the TV cameras zoomed so that viewers could look into

the shaman mask of her ruined face. 'I'll tell you High John's
meaning for us,' came that growly voice, speaking Ma Johnson's
words to the viewers: 'Make wealth, for others. Don't imagine
that if you live selfish, somehow wealth will grow generous in
your land. First, comes the change in your spirit. Don't you go
to the Right. They say: 'The rest of humanity lives in sin;
so keep *our* taxes low, crack down on crime, fill the prisons,
take the babies of the wicked and put them in camps.' Don't you go

to the Clintonists. They say: 'We're all in this together, but...
with a social service boost, things as they are, better budget
management...our society works, dammit, this is a great country!'
Don't you go to the Liberals. They say: 'Raise taxes from the wealthy.
Don't lavish it on the poor – those the 'inadequate, idle' poor!'
Don't you go to Revolutionaries, minds full of hell. They say:
'We, we are pure!' – mouth full of righteousness, gut
full of cruelty! Don't fall for Single Issues: Feminists, the Poor

even. Gays, Abortion Rightists. They say: 'Solve this one issue
and the world will be transformed.' No doubt. But it's a tissue
of lies to think one issue will do it. Don't you go
to Anarchists: self-will ain't no social ethic. No,
all solutions are false when the spirit is wrong: the biggest mistake
of our age is to think politics will cure our lives. I know
High John fought this one evil' – and she wept – 'How we miss you,
High John – you never believed your wealth was your own, that mistake

the rest of this goddamned nation makes daily. We – I say we –
spent multi-billions bailing out white-run, Congress-friendly
savings and loans banks, while the Freedom Bank of Harlem (which fed
new firms into *that* heartland) needed six million but was left for dead–
'The Feds will pay half' – does that make you laugh? A white cloud
fogs the national mind, 'spite what the national mouth has said
in all its prudent pity...What didja burn' bout, Bush? Tellin' me
some god-father trooths from yr White White White House smoke-cloud?'

Like a whitened oasis of light in the cemetery gloom, the debate
took place amid spreadeagled crowds, half of whom sat
on funerary slabs, the TV trolleys a Martian incursion
to and fro. The audience at home heard clearest – their version
came with a Peter Belia voice-over: indeed 'the Belly'
idled, mike in hand, by a tombstone, his angle mere subversion
of all that the party stood for: 'Spirit is politically isolate
during its greatest tragedy, its martyrdom,' broadcast 'the Belly'.

'We know these things,' came a Robeson voice from a cloud of rainbow
robes now alongside Dolores. Lifting her gently by the elbow,
the man helped her from the grave – call him Mr Rainbow, a coalition-
minded pol from Flatbush, strong on tradition, but who was wishin',
despite all that Peter Belia had claimed, for alliance with Spirit
at this cross-point of martyrdom. 'We have Muslims, Marxists, Christian
salvationists down in Flatbush,' Rainbow said, 'but below
the high-flying rap, we're working hard, not so unlike Spirit.'

'Mr Rainbow,' spat the preacherman, 'You're just too darned amicable
for anyone's good. Spirit now faces *us* – its Islamic radical
alternative.' Will, hand in hand with Emen, came to the graveside
where High John, lying still, still was the motion beneath each side
of debate. Rainbow stood aside while their Islamic opponent,
sharp-eyed, no taller than Dolores, charged: 'That Belia hasn't lied.
Your movement hasn't gone deep: think you've got City Hall
worried? Drug lords! Ha! Come down to earth, we's your real opponent.

For you're just new immigrants, some whiteys, some quiet-living oldsters,
like Ma Johnson from Harlem, some Asians, ain't no guns in them holsters
that I can see. You got nuttin' to say to the Black activists,
no Day of Outrage among your thinking, don't see no Marxists,
or one of our lawyers or reverends to fan the flames into heat.
You certain you got angry enough? Or 're you just quietists
of the usual kind, wondering what the next day's opinion pollsters
are going to say of your party? Sure, Dolores here got the heat–

we honor you, Dolores – but you can't run politics on morals. You need
political theory, Black religion, history, anger, and a new breed
of citizen, something of a swagger in yos walk.' 'Yeah, yeah, you talk,'
returned Dolores, 'but 's two hunnered thousand businesses in New York
only fifteen hunnered black-owned: where *theory*, where religion,
where anger in that? Gonna boycott another Korean grocery? Walk
how you like, but if you not gonna buy back your city from the greed
of whites, you not talking real: so don't trust to no creepy religion,

Mister.' 'Listen, sister,' intervened Mr Rainbow, with a frown,
'You've never heard of GIFT – that's Garvey Income for Tomorrow – down
in Flatbush, where they've bought 74 Kenilworth Place by pooling
Black *re*sources, taking out shares? So they're not fooling
around like you say; they're gonna open up stores one at a time,
cost so far's three hundred thou'. They don't need any schooling
from you – didn't Marcus Garvey get 'em buying factories, and one
time a steamship line in the twenties?' At last, Emen's long time

of mournful silence ended, though her voice stayed throaty, as she
lifted her own black veil: 'We'd give gift for gift, as long as the
males haven't any *fixed solutions* to impose on the rest of us.
You going to be that humble in politics or religion? Don't bother us
if not. And what are these robes – the rainbow coalition?
Few too many male politicians in that for us
to cohabit with happily! Everyone staying in fixed tracks: that's fantasy
politics, hard edges to stripes in your 'rainbow coalition'.

Deadlock. A TV technician switched out a light and, bored,
rejoined his producer – the camera panning over that graveyard
of non-consensus: rainbow robes swirled amidst tombstones, while masculine
pride wanted – not that there be a *solution*, but to be the *politician*
that knew it. So radical warred with peacemaker – the boxers left,
other details inessential – for now a man took up the feminine
cause, the one man without right; it was Will who came forward,
white, new immigrant, poet not politician. 'Now they've left,'

he said, 'I am going to speak on matters I am debarred from
by every sacred rule of justice, for I represent the problem,
the evil one, the oppressor, in his weakest form: I'm the penniless
envoy of moneyed power, a poet now utterly poem-less
to hear this buzz of counter-dialectics: racial-universal,
majority-minority, minority-minority, creed-creedless,
patriarchy-matriarchy. All's trapped in a web. Where is the poem
that High John's spirit can inspire with the truly Universal?'

Poetry? And not even Black poetry? And on such a subject!
A huge and derisive laugh swept the cemetery at this abject
white male whom Emen, too, was grinning at. Undeterred, Will
continued: 'Without a yielding white voice – and that a male
one – we shall not achieve the uproarious incantation
which alone will rouse Spirit. I bow to your honors, as I tell
you that only a transcendent, angelic spirit can unite dialectic
without outright war. It comes! Ah, finally! This is my incantation:

Will's Incantation

I see the Jewish Christess rise with black Judaic skin
thick lips of a Sicilian, and she speaks Islamic Puerto Rican words
in an Irish brogue, her cheeks and eyebrows plumped out
in Koreanesque-Japanesoid narrowness, and she fingers
her fortune-cookie testicles as she speaks,
the prick rising like that of a messiahness,
a lion prick in a lioness
more ambiguous in sex than Voodoo's Legba
more thunderous than the Yoruban Shango
her peace palm in air,
mutated seven fingers like branches
of a minorah, or like a Buddha's enlightened palm,
or the fingers of Shiva,
and she is also atheist,
and she is rising in a stable of origin.

Oh Lord – Who is Lord? – Oh Lordess
you are the bridegroom to Justess,
which is female, a black mare of night,
arise in your stable, Christess,
in your groom's leather leggings arise:
provide the stirrup that burns
under the instep of the jockeys of night
riding the black night mares
shadows racing down the lost perspectives of street lamps
past burning automobiles of darkness
fires in the streets of lost civil rights
the race of invisibles down lanes alternative to the fast lanes
dearborn angel in black
angel more than us arise from politics of contest
not to end contest, but to add spurs and stirrups
to the one, true race of our time.
Come to this stable, Judaic Christess
from your Italo-Irish Protestant cathedrals,
take at last the white wafers of guilt from my mouth
my tongue coated as if with thrush
in my sorrow-song at those we have outlawed
who die on the margins, in garishly-lit hospices
or in African countries stricken with plagues;
come and saddle my stallion of justice
with the female; let the dead ancestors, feminine/
masculine, rise from the straw and fill me
with their strange coffin energies, till

bestride my mare at the stable's very door
I sense the spirits of past lives
arise and mount their saddled stallions
or saddled mares
and the groom, the Christess, rising,
mounts her own ambi-sexual mare
to head us out in processional
under the startling readiness of stars
to move and alter heavenly pattern.

Inhabitants ride out from side streets,
in readiness to join us and change their fates,
leaving the overturned automobiles
which make the air stink with vanquished power.
Until at a crossroads the horse of the Christess
leading us, rears, paws the ground, impatient
to start down the last straight
of this race towards human-ness and meaning of lives
this almost possible track directly ahead
beyond Western horizons,
where we would be jockeyesses
our pricks frotted on our feminine animals
turning their wild black heads as if to suck at our shuddering breasts.

When I come there may my mare, too,
paw and rear at those crossroads of choice,
for the true cross unites all religions;
it is the entirely free choice, the zen moment of spirit,
the darkness of center-non-center in all metaphysics,
and atheist astrophysics.
Right there in the non-mid-point, rear, my mare of night
saddled by the Christess, your dark groom,
and then light out for dead ahead,
the air crackling with spirits around,
my stirrups in flames round my shoe soles,
everything suddenly obvious:
the crabby males
that run nations, wrongly voted in,
wrongly voted in –
left behind in the ruin of their cities.
Here, over the horizon rim in a darker darkness,
a new world out of the western old one
riders hugging the necks of animals running,
black flanks flickering with lights.

He finished, turned to the one TV camera still operating, and despite
the producer's reluctance to keep filming, gave a great shout,
in Latin – Marlowe's Ovidian tag, 'Slowly, slowly,
ride, you horses of the night', but changing this to 'swiftly':
Celeriter, celeriter, currite noctis equi!...
...Silence
followed! What happened next has entered the annals of party
history. Emen, changed from her widow's weeds, came out
of the crowd her face rapt – possessed, some said. Silence!

She had donned fancy clothes, male clothes, out of spaghetti East-
ern tradition: fly-away leather riding coat, a vest
of red velvet, plump leather jeans, platform boots, and over
her ears was hooked a false beard – the full chest coverer
kind of Karl Marx. Her head, by means of a bisected pink
balloon was made white-man hairy-bald, a buffoon above her
black cheeks, and the whites of her eyes were showing. Impressed,
the TV team zoomed in on the balloon, so that viewers saw pink.

Now changes of clothes are common in Voodoo possession, and Will
and Emen had planned this charade. But there came an electronic wail
from the feminine lips of this black grandee, deliciously shiversome
a wail in what Voodoo calls *langage*, a speak known to no one,
the words of possession. Waiting with his mike, Belia was grinning
impishly. 'Pardon me,' he began, 'but do I address you as someone
with a definite sex, or is that question, er-hum, best left well
alone?' A high cheekbone in her face caught a gleam, and, grinning

back at Belia, the figure disclosed under its chin
an electronic voicebox, whose grille bleated in feminine
tone of an Indian, a Japanese, a Spaniard – or some other:
'*Mis amigos han obrado con poco tino y con menos politica...*'
it said. '*No es verdad?*' asked Belia, and added: '*Véro?*'
because a Sicilian shrug had followed the Spanish phrase.
'*Il senso più comune di 'che' non e il più véro... – Hélas,
il serait bien nécessaire de souligner...Excusez-moi...*' '*Véro?*'

asked Belia, falling one Panurgian language behind. '*Nga nsibidi
adohe – aku natongena wud nsibidi... Excusez-moi. Sthiti-
prabhāvasukhadyutileśyāviśuddhīndriyā-
vadhiviṣayato adhikāh.*' Like all the new born, the figure
had trouble beginning to speak. '*Strobodi nkta homongas katit
kordovi plan*' (East European, say Siberian, dialect?) 'I'd rather
we spoke English for the viewers,' chuckled Belia. 'Weren't we
discussing what sex you were?' 'My rider in me is complicated,'

came a *femina perturba* voice in English – rider being a usual
Voodoo term for the loa. 'I'm not bisexual, but all-sexual,
he-she-she-he originating together in unique desires. Not African
desires, or Waspy ones, or Asian, or Hispanic, or Amerindian:
I contains all of esh, differences held separately, separate in unity,
held in each flash of personality like facets of the one
personality: think of a painting whose colors are individual
but simultaneously perceived, separate in brilliance, formal in unity.'

'Esh?' queried Belia. 'Ms. Rider, is that your name?' 'I am Hooman.'
'So is 'esh' one of those feminist pronouns?' 'My nominative pronoun
is Esh – pronounce it not carefully like a name, but careless-
ly as in 'h'does this' – 'Sh'does this' – or with Esh – ''shdoes this'.
I am Esh from out of the Yoruban Eshu-Ellegbara, cognate
with Voodoo's Legba, a nimble she in reverse. Objective case:
Em – it suggests mE backwards and also my horse, Emen.
The possessive nominal's Eshine (for the nominal must become cognate

with shining – the self-possession that shines). Possessive attributive,
Sher (in generous possession Esh shares what is Eshine). To give
me a name, as a Hooman, I am 'Thus Spirit', 'Thus' being my equivalent
for Mr or Ms. Or call me Hoo.' 'Well,' ironized Belia, 'that's ambivalent
enough for anyone! And you seem a rational spirit! There are things
going on I don't understand.' 'Some things can't be understood in virulent
moods, Mr Belia,' Hooman's voice suddenly said. Belia paled as if
a steel blade had cleaved through his soul. It was one of those things

that can't be explained: entire authority exercised without force.
'Suppose you become yourself, Mr Belia,' said this courteous,
possessed woman, face eshining, so that viewers saw the Good there,
transcendental in Emen's own skin – 'yourself but also your neighbor
humans on Earth imagined vividly – vividness, the vital quality
of a mind that unites with goodness in a rush of warm feeling, a quiver
of warmth stabbing like fear. In that instant, your sex or your race
is both sexes, all races, yet one and your own – heightened in quality.

Je suis comme ça! And how can I tolerate another's poverty or exclusion
when I see it so vividly as my own in them? This is ur-dimension
empathy I'm talking about, a possibility you fourth dimensional creatures
are powerless against.' Emen's changes of physical features
were rapid, a confusing of forms in the beholder's eye, yet a stable
identity both frightened the heart and warmed it. No speech is
adequate to say this truth firmly enough: when Emen's Good became vision
vividly enough, it was blindingly obvious; the most detestable

of humanity's failing is refusal to open the iris to that Good,
and Hoo emself was that vision, riding Emen who had humbly stood
aside while Will chanted, until her gaze dimmed and the loa's weight
descended on her back, and she'd writhed, and spoken in the inchoate
synthesized words of her voice-box. Then gathering around Hooman
came the Black activists – cameras still whirring, the program was running
late – but back in the studios the program chief, enchanted, could
not cut it short: for Emen was so photogenic, ridden by Hooman.

'Yes, I invoked you, Hooman,' Will called. 'You are us collectively
speaking: the Present, the Voodooed Present, but even more lively
than spirit possession, esh's the dance of the Present in space-time,
Esh's the Presidance, the Presidente, the President al dente, the sublime
moment when hard becomes soft, sexually, socially, politically, open.
Pardon me, I'm a poet, I got carried away with the beauty of rhyme.'
Belia, the memorious, blurted out: 'But there's something here olden time.
Doesn't Esh look like Gouverneur Morris, whose radical aristo pen

framed the final draft of our Constitution? (Morrisania's first notable
now bearded transnational, transsexual, viewers.)' Tripping on his cable
he lurched into camera...So as the studio grumbles, 'I don't know why,
we're doing this segment', we leave the cemetery and enter some family
lounge with the TV on and the face of Hoo looming, the kids bellowing
to change channels but, oddly, that doesn't happen. And the sides
of the set frame the face stagily, the pale crowd in the shadowy
background like secondary actors, and the night like tent walls billowing.

At Emen's throat, the voice-box spat and took over again:

'DECLARATION,

'When in the Course of Hooman events it becomes necessary for one
people to dissolve the political bands which have connected them with
another, and to assume among the powers of the earth, the separate
and equal station to which the Laws of Nature and of Nature's Godd-ess
entitle them, a decent respect to the opinions of Hoomankind requires
that they should declare the causes which impel them to the separation.
– We hold these truths to be self-evident, that all Hoomans are created
equal, that they are endowed by their Creator with certain unalienable
Rights, that among these are Life, Liberty and the pursuit of Happiness.
– That to secure these rights, Governments are instituted among
Hoomans, deriving their just powers from the consent of the governed,
– That whenever any Form of Government becomes destructive of
these ends, it is the Right of the People to alter or to abolish it, and
to institute new Government, laying its foundation on such principles

and organizing its powers in such form, as to them shall seem most likely to effect their Safety and Happiness. Prudence, indeed, will dictate that Governments long established should not be changed for light and transient causes. But when a long train of abuses and usurpations of the democratic processes, in which the powerful and wealthy pursuing invariably the same Object evince a design to reduce any considerable number of people under absolute Despotism, it is their right, it is their duty, to modify such Government, and to provide new Guards for their future security.

Such has been the patient sufferance of the A1 Congressional District, New York State, of these United States; and, though despotism has disguised itself in the cloak of democracy, yet it has condemned us to the meanest conditions of survival, and has refused to acknowledge in Congress the interests of this District, judged in recent times the poorest of all Congressional Districts in these States. And this great evil has arisen partly out of historical circumstance of immigration and slavery, but more particularly out of the establishment of absolute tyranny over the electoral processes of these States by two powerful political groupings: what has been called the military-industrial complex; and the seizure of the nation's financial resources into the private hands of impersonal corporations, of greedy and ambitious families, and of financial entrepreneurs. That Government should not stand long, for which the majority of an electorate, in its disgust at the briberies and the toadying time-serving of its alleged representatives, has ceased to vote at all. In this desertion of a people from its electoral duty, elites may lead whole nations into immoral behavior. We declare that President effectually a tyrant who, voted in by 20% of an electorate, supported in policy by Congressional majority representing little more than one third of the electorate, and – scantly heeding even that popular mandate but swaying a nation by lies and political manipulation – enters into a cabal with a few nearest friends, his own appointees, to commit our own hands to the bloody sacrifice of soldiers and civilians in foreign nations. Meanwhile, the powerful have made themselves secure in their local and national offices, ensuring through clumsy laws that the uneducated will be deterred from electoral registration and that only those faithful to party elites, or to the military complex, or to the private wealth of corporations or individuals, may succeed in presenting a political platform fully before any electorate. Particularly, we would protest at the overweening size of these United States, measured not only in land mass but also in population, so that any individual voice crying for justice in the wastelands of urban deprivation cries utterly in vain; any larger group cries in vain; knowing that Congress has ceased to represent the needs of the poor and disadvantaged.

Such great evil may not persist without the opposition of all honorable Hoomans. It is to address the effectual tyranny of elites and of all political Machiavellianism that we reluctantly combine to change, unilaterally, our allegiance to the laws under which we are governed. We are yet gravely mindful of the dangers of civil warfare that may result from acts of secession, and so we voluntarily rescind our natural right to rebel absolutely against all absolute tyranny; and still we, the disenfranchised of District A1, New York State, United States of America, act to save ourselves from remaining the *de facto* slaves of that richer nation comprised of the whole United States themselves. We have determined to live by the dictates of a new Constitution, so to be an exemplar for our nation, how a peaceful people composed of many races can live harmoniously together on much smaller a scale, denying money for militaristic causes, denying the runaway reign of greed, and electing our own President and Congress out of new laws existing, as it were, in parenthesis to the old ones. All legal consequences of our actions incurred by us under the provisions of the original, broader Constitution will be suffered by us peacefully and patiently, for we would be model citizens. We have confidence that Justice itself is self-evident in its Truthfulness; and that a nation brought up from its earliest days to respect Democracy and Justice will hardly look unfavorably upon this Little Nation within the Larger Nation, since our whole wish is a return to those ideals perverted into financial considerations, and into a permission for slavery, by the original framers of our liberties.

We hereby proclaim our own governing Constitution:

At the throat, the black voice-box crackled, and bled a last
phrase: 'The new Constitution's been stored on disks, which we'll pass
around now.' Then, like one who'd been stabbed in the jugular,
Emen went rigid, with stretched chin; suddenly her regalia
looked ridiculous, and she shivered white-eyed, tongue pushed
out, her knees knocking; her hands in jerky irregular
gestures produced from her clothes and scattered all over the grass
a slew of computer disks; and she fell as if brutally pushed.

Lou Levinson, the lawyer, rushed to her: in a second, he'd found
a piece of paper tucked in her breasts. 'Let me lie on the ground
while my loa leaves me,' he read out. 'The rest of you stand back.
These disks will be sent to the Press. Load them into a Mac
Classic computer, but expect no screen display; everything's on audio
synthesized through the sound system. Don't try to back
up the disk or you'll lose everything. To capture the sound,
take an ordinary acoustic recorder and record it direct on audio.'

The TVs faded in each living room, as the transfixed producer
at last threw the switch and, hastily calm, the studio announcer
excused the length of the funeral segment. But the switchboard reported
a significant number of callers who asked that the aborted
coverage of Esh and Emen be resumed. The 11 p.m. news
only referred to High John's boxing career, so, thwarted,
the callers turned on their local newspapers to produce a
full story on the new Constitution as front-page news.

The callers were soothed to be told that by cross-national Express
Mail similar disks had been sent already to the Press,
who had set up their Macs. And this is what happened. Once in its drive,
the disk caused the computers to speak (screens blank). Anyone who tried
to copy the disk would see this message: 'Warning: a virus
will attack your hard drive if you continue.' So only the 'live'
recording survived, because, once the voice finished, a new mess-
age appeared. 'Disk being initialized (rubbed out) thanks to our virus.'

(Spirit would later claim that Emen's 'rider', the Legba
composite, in a move of surprising modernity for a Voodoo loa,
had projected the program on to the disks, but the Supreme Court
was to throw this claim out with great scorn.) Only a brief report
of what the voice said may follow: for the whole new U.S. Constitution,
as spoken through the computers, can't be relayed in the short
span of these verses. So we'll confine ourselves to the changes, to a
stripped-down account of Spirit's new U.S. Constitution:

CONSTITUTION OF DISTRICT A1, NEW YORK STATE, UNITED STATES OF AMERICA

PREAMBLE

We, the people of District A1, New York State, in the United States of America, having come to understand that the original Union of these United States has outgrown the Constitution of its setting out, do ordain and establish a newly reformed Constitution. We do so not in disrespect to our forebears, who wished to create a great nation out of the diverse peoples of the Earth but who could not have foreseen the vast growth of an oversized nation; rather we act in culmination of their wishes, aware that no set of words is so utterly sacred that it can endure for ever or subsist in truthfulness merely through addition and amendment.

Beginning again in small compass, we proclaim the setting up of a more perfect union and a more equitable Justice. We shall insure an end to Corrupt Ways, make different provision for the common defence, promote the general Welfare through smaller groupings of peoples, and thus secure domestic Tranquillity and renew the Blessings of Liberty to ourselves and our Posterity.'

(And these are the main changes):

Section

1. The Constitution first adopted by District A1 (a pro-tem Congressional District of New York State), eventually to be changed for adoption by the necessary majority of the whole United States electorate.

2. Establishment of Congresses at three levels: old Congressional Districts, State, and National (with special arrangements for major urban centers).

3. All executive power, save that of signing Bills of National Congress into Law, to be stripped from President and Vice-President of the United States, who become ceremonial heads of the Nation.

4. An end to the easily corruptible system of primary and full elections for Presidential and Congressional offices, to the multiplicity of elections for local administrative offices, and to the Presidential power to appoint any but sher own advisory and office staff, who shall have no other powers. Replacing such systems is a single series of elections through popular plebiscite at each level, beginning with that for District President, Vice-President, Representatives, and Senators (chosen from among Representatives). Only those holding such District offices will be eligible for election to the same offices at State level. Only those holding such State offices will be eligible for election to the same offices at National level. Candidates' campaigns to be limited to means provided by District, State, and National government as appropriate. Some weeding-out of candidates may be necessary by popularly elected Boards, but within strict limits. All candidates for administrative offices to be appointed after public advertisement of the posts by Boards selected by the appropriate Congress.

5. Where the original Constitution reads 'life, liberty, and possessions' this be modified to 'life, liberty, and those possessions which do not create egregious hoardings of individual wealth expressed as proportions of the national average wealth as elsewhere defined in this Present Constitution.'

6. All Bills shall originate in either the House of Representatives or the Senate, or by vote of the Electorate through plebiscite. Plebiscites shall be limited to not more than one each year and a two-thirds majority of the electorate shall be necessary before a Bill originating in such a fashion be presented to the Congress of this District. (Save only that the words 'he' shall read 'esh', 'his' shall read 'sher', and 'him' shall

read 'em', and being made applicable to this District, this Section follows the wording of Article I, Section 6, of the Original Constitution and is taken as read.)

7. Powers of the National Congress will include:

   (a) To concentrate by whatever legal means necessary the main interest of the United States upon the concerns of other nations in the world to achieve a better Planet Earth and a fairer and more conservative use of global resources. Government has the Duty to take such legislative action even against the narrower national interests of the United States, whose citizens henceforth regard themselves as world citizens before they are national citizens.

   (b) (To raise Armies, a Navy, an Airforce, a Militia, etc. as in the Original Constitution, but limited as stated in the provisions of the Present Constitution.)

   (c) To lay and collect Taxes, Duties, Imposts and Excises, to pay the Debts and provide for the common Defense and general Welfare of the Unites States; but all Duties, Imposts and Excises shall be uniform throughout the United States. All levying for military expenditure will be submitted to national plebiscite every two years in six alternative, itemized lists bearing the following proportions to each other expressed as percentages of highest cost: 5%, 20%, 40%, 60%, 80%, 100%.

   (d) To enforce phasing out of all nuclear-based armaments. To ban all sale or use of armaments outside the geographical borders of the United States, except where essential to national defense when War has been Declared by National Congress.

   (e) To ally the United States of America absolutely with all peaceful decisions of the United Nations, where passed by due process of the Laws of the United Nations. Any decisions of the United Nations involving wars to be subject to the National Laws relating to warfare, as outlined above.

   (f) To define and to punish any scientific experiments or commercial activities that are judged by Committee of the National Administration inhumane or detrimental to the interests of Citizens of the Planet Earth, its Atmosphere, or to the Regions of Outer Space.

   (g) To limit monopolies and to curb any expenditure of money by private individuals, or by private, public, or foreign clubs, firms, organizations, or corporations, or by foreign nations designed to influence unfairly the governmental, political, or democratic processes of the United Sates or to interfere with its elections.

   (h) To declare a state of Official Dispute with multinational clubs, firms, corporations, or foreign governments if they engage in activities detrimental to United States interests, and to press for the strengthening of international legal means to settle such disputes.

(i) To borrow Money on the credit of the United States, provided that these sums when added to total present borrowings do not exceed half the previous year's gross national product. These provisions shall take no account of borrowings already made at the time this Constitution may be adopted for the whole of the United States.

(j) To establish an Administration of Incomes Estimates (A.I.E.) to define and measure the wealth of individuals and of private firms and corporations and to report the results to the Nation at least every three years. To levy such taxation that will ensure that no private individual shall earn an average annual income of more than eight times the national average, as most recently measured by the A.I.E. While existing holdings of private wealth may not be immediately attacked, it is understood that Congress will endeavor within such time as is consonant with sufficient national prosperity to reduce all holdings of private wealth to no more than ten times the national average holdings, as most recently measured by the A.I.E., while firms, organizations, and corporations will be rigorously controlled and if necessary their officers punished to prevent all attempts to evade these aforesaid restrictions upon private wealth.

(k) To decree what forms of transport are allowable in the United States and to regulate and facilitate such transports as may be needful while suppressing those forms which may not be needful having due regard to the prosperity and happiness of citizens of the United States and of the Planet Earth.

(l) To review the distribution of happiness, opportunity, and prosperity throughout the United States and, not tolerating any notorious injustice between Congressional Districts in any such distribution, to undertake such measures as may be necessary to restore a more equitable balance and to create favorable environments for the health, and educational and moral development of the young people of the United States.

8. Where any of the foregoing provisions in Sections 1-7 are in conflict with provisions of the Original Constitution of the United States of America the foregoing provisions are deemed to be the higher authority.

(Otherwise, the Original Constitution will be modified to accord its detailed provisions with any discordances it creates with the Present Constitution.)

To those Amendments to the Original Constitution known as the Human Rights Amendments the following shall be added:

(a) Notwithstanding Section 7(b) of the Present Constitution, any United States Citizen shall have the right to withhold such measure of sher taxes as may be assigned to the creation of armaments or to the maintenance of armies. The right of self-defense being unalienable and natural to every Hooman, in all matters regarding the raising of armies or militias or regarding the Declaration of Wars for the common Defense of the whole United States, it shall lie within the authority of each individual member of the electorate of this District to agree or not to agree to participate in such armies, militias, or wars, without let or hindrance from any fellow citizen or any group, organization, or governmental body whatsoever. Where this provision of the present paragraph creates a contradiction under Law with the Original Constitution of the United States, this same paragraph of the Present Constitution shall be deemed the higher authority under Law.

(b) Article II of the Amendments to the Original Constitution (right of the people to keep and bear arms) is hereby annulled.

On a dull news day six factors held sway: High John's career,
his martyrdom, the successes of Spirit, a whiff of Voodoo, the sheer
weirdness of Emen's 'voice' and fancy dress, and, a bit,
the novelty of the Constitution – what would the Feds do about it,
since it ranked as an act of secession, albeit only by one
Congressional District? Oh, and anyway, what District? Spirit
had said 'A1', which didn't exist. Columnists thought it near
the Bronx neighborhood; but: 'Spirit's HQ is Brooklyn,' said one.

The Feds sneered and sent their most Ancient of Days, Joe Fedora,
to check the Bronx. His car on idle, Joe groaned when he saw a
huge wall billboard: 'District A1 secedes from the Union by a hundred
per cent majority. The new U.S.A. starts here!' He wondered
if that was the only poster; so before taking action he continued
towards Brooklyn Bridge, already hungry for lunch, but he blundered
into a score of posters West Side – East Side many more, a
white plague of them Downtown. '*Dio mio*! What next?' He continued

to a precinct where cops were asking the question: how'd they succeeded
in posting those posters unnoticed? What district had seceded
and in what voting session, where? Joe Fedora found it all worse
than investigating the Teamsters: no one would mutter more than a terse
'Ask at Spirit's headquarters on Utica, Brooklyn.' And at that HQ
the bosses were missing – just more citizens. Yes, worse than the Mafia's
silence, because thousands of people seemed involved. Though hope receded
of finding out more, Joe set up surveillance 'cross the street from HQ.

The Feds had a stroke of luck. Ma Johnson moved in next door
to Joe's surveillance post. 'Af-am – FBI? You're
kidding if those became friends!' Well, we're not. No sex though, for Joe
was a closet gay from the Hoover era of gays. And lo
and behold, Ma proved voluble but vague. She implied that something
was going down in the Bronx – Morrisania on some Wednesday, scenario
hazy – a waste plot, an election for President – 'Ah don' know mo':
A huge votin' session on some hot ballotin' machines, or sump'in'–,

load o' nonsense, if you aks me.' The Feds staked out Morrisania
and Washington gave Joe a back-up team. What was even zanier
for the Feds, a tacit agreement had somehow been struck by numerous
taxpayers across the U.S. not to pay taxes for defense.
The Treasury raised a fuss but thought that the threat of prison
would bring most protesters to heel. More worrying was the anonymous
way the movement had spread, though Spirit was certainly a
prime suspect for conspiracy to hide crime. A charge of misprision

was laid against Emen, who simply replied that the loa had spoken
through her while she'd been unconscious, and that when she'd awoken
the disk that created the voice at her throat – initialized
before the ceremony to be clean for the voice that had surprised
a nation of viewers – had auto-destructed like those they had sent
to the Press. 'Listen, Man,' said her cheeky letter to the wise-
guy Treasury lawyer, 'our party's called Spirit: by that token
we mean we invoke it. We have no control on when it is present.'

In New York, the drivers of cars would report to the cops that a wall
of women – now famous as Spirit's main tactic – had stopped all
traffic from entering such and such a district. But no rhyme
or reason connected these incidents which lasted for such a short time
that the police on arrival found the streets empty, with the local squad
car blocked in on all sides so the doors wouldn't open – but no crime
really involved. This was a puzzle. Then there'd follow a call
to the precinct to say that easy arrests awaited the drug squad,

as some dealers were locked in their crack pads – the locals had instant
devices to bar doors and windows; they could seal up a basement
from round corners so the crackheads couldn't get off a shot. The police
called these areas 'the Brigadoon No-Gos', but whether designed to decrease
drug traffic or the ordinary motorists' waste of world fuel
resources was unclear. Assembling a case was hard. In the first place
many had worn masks; second, the locksmiths who'd obviously lent
the bars all said they'd turned a blind eye – been a bit of a fool.

At last someone brighter on the Mayor's staff said, 'Listen: these assholes
are laying their plans; they're not moral crusaders – they're pols
just like us. All this war on gasoline is just their asshole routine
and so are the drug busts. We'll go wrong if we think they don't mean
what they say: this is Constitutional, Secessional, a little more serious
than we supposed. I'd guess that when they wall off a street they convene
a planning meeting – a no-go area so's to leave no loopholes
for us to spy on them: we should now tell Capitol Hill this is serious.'

So the Feds got leant on again. Now how does a Fed know how to act
like a Fed? From his colleagues? Well, how do they? In fact,
part of their manners and lingo they learn from the movies, and part
from organized crime, which also learns from the movies; so art
without spirit has an effect on real life. The FBI
buzzed warnings to all agents to step up surveillance, to get dirt
on Spirit's leaders, to check their crime records, to contact
the local IRS, try for sex scandals – yes, this, the Hollywood FBI.

'Well, I am aksing *you*, Ma,' parodied Joe one day, very frustrated,
for he was taking a lot of heat. 'I'm a Fed –
should've told you that before.' 'Oh no!' wailed Ma Johnson throwing
a stage fit. 'What's all that I've bin tellin' you 'bout what's goin'
down in stolen ballot machines? 'Taint none of it true, d'you hear?
I'm not saying nothing more to a Fed: you check Charlotte Street,
won't find no thing there till the day – but what am ah sayin'?
None of it's true. We'll ballot away just in thin air, d'you hear?'

The FBI told Joe: 'Check it.' So, while a partner glued
his eyes to the binocs, he went to a bar where he met a lewd
eye contact from the gay Jewish lawyer, Lou Levinson, who invited
him to his table and eventually back to his pad. 'Don't get excited,'
said Joe, 'I haven't yet said who I am.' 'Yes you have,' said the lawyer,
'without meaning to. You're the Fed on surveillance. Really, I'm delighted
to meet you…just doing your job and so forth. And I shan't be crude,
sweetie, I see you're too old for me' – added that gay lawyer.

'I'm speaking little difficulties, Lou,' said Joe, all pinpoint-
eyed. 'We found a yellow notepad on your desk – get the point?
Yes, a draft of this Constitution thing – shall we say 'sedition'
or 'treason', or 'conspiracy to avoid defense tax?' Now I mention
tax, Lou, shall I refer to the undervalued stock sale
on your '87 return? Yes, we raided your offices – I had a notion
we might find something – huh! wuz no need to turn the joint
over – wuz all in plain view. Now what you got for sale

in return for a plea bargain, I wonder, 'cos *we* got *you* in a squeeze?'
And squeezed Lou did look, his cheeks gone pale. 'I'll talk, but please
understand my loyalties here to Spirit,' said the stoolie, with unctuous
morality up for offer. And Joe understood all too well with a gracious
and ironical nod. 'What I want,' said the Fed, 'ain't too hard to give.
Jest a date an' a time for this cockamamie Constitutional caucus,
convention, whatever, that's comin' up. Don't spill the whole beanz,
no names or nuffin', jest a date, I say: that ain't hard to give.'

Lou stared at Joe's tie-pin: 'I bet you've a bug; you're all wired,'
and he laughed nervously. Then he rose, dragged down by newly-acquired
disloyalty, went to a wall calendar, pointed silently to a date;
next to a map of New York where he showed Joe a waste plot
in the Bronx, shot a cuff and swivelled the hands on his watch
to 11 a.m., finishing off with a little playlet
of a voter voting at a ballot machine, glancing sideways, scared.
Lou gave the shrug of bad faith, sat again, and watched Joe watch

him with those narrowed eyes. The lack of sex in this scene will be
remarked. Nothing here of 'Lou on top,' or of 'Joe willingly
accepting the masculine sperm', here where Federal and District
stayed at loggerheads, symptom of a national failure to conscript
the local into a wider, fairer political process – a failure of law
and of justice, so it seemed. We'll let Joe leave and phone his transcript
of these proceedings to Washington, where the powers that be
sent agents into Morrisania, and studied their Constitutional law.

On the eve of the poll, they called Joe in for debriefing: the assistant
under-deputy chief Fed, an administration deputy head of department,
a police superintendent from the Bronx, and a Treasury official
halfway up the hierarchy – Spirit was a problem but not a huge social
issue. 'Zeze guys ain't doin' nuttin' hefty yet,' Joe agreed
with the Admin man. 'But jeeze organized, yes. An' that Haitian'll
charm the pants off a peacock. They're going to lead us on a dance,
election day, take us the wrong way. It's been agreed

by hundreds maybe thousands of 'em to take the wrong subway outto
Brooklyn, throw us off the scent; then at 11 a.m. double back to
Morrisania for the poll. This checks out three, four times,
I tellya.' 'So what've we got?' asked Treasury. 'We got names, seems
we got date, time, place, we got stake-out by that plot
in Morrisania, agents on the subways ready, and major league teams
o' cops. We got the lot.' It all broke up with 'Well done, Joe,'
and a call to New York's Mayor, with full details of the plot.

That Wednesday morning, Ma Johnson opened her door a crack
at 6 a.m., and Joe was listening; he softly followed her out the back
of the block and on to the subway platform, packed with people going
to Seventh Avenue, Brooklyn, he guessed gleefully, his face glowing
with pride at a job well done. 'You ain't foolin' me,' he secretly
told those crowds. While Ma waited, he huddled by a news stand and knowing
what to expect put a walkie-talkie to his ear. Great! A large shack
had appeared overnight on the Morrisania waste plot, and secretly,

the Black Activist allies like emergency medics carrying stretchers
had imported long packages in brown paper wrappings. Stretches
of ground were being cleared and marked in white tape for the voting
lines. O.K. Joe back in Brooklyn watched Ma and the others entering
the F train then climbed in a bulging car: out at Seventh
and a walk uphill with a large enough crowd for the Yankees trying
for the World Series. He admired, as a pro, these nice touches
in Spirit's plans, everyone idling before rushing back to Seventh

and taking the subway to the Bronx. As the morning was still quite dark
it took him a while to get uneasy. Not till they neared Prospect Park
did he notice everyone changing direction, the approach roads
become blocked by people lying down and the rest in hordes
entering the park. At least 10,000 and probably more.
His beeper sounded – the Brooklyn cops were trying to make inroads
across the bodies of peaceful citizens – sounded again and he barked
to the Bronx agents, 'Call off the Sting – Round 'em up, any more

come your way arrest 'em. We got problems.' (To finish the Bronx story,
they raided the shack to find the activists mocking an effigy
many feet high of the President – the real president, we should say –
though if wealth decides who is real, there's the devil to pay.
Suddenly, in Brooklyn, 7.55, everyone started running
from side roads uphill to the park, cops among them, as the first ray
of the sun broke over the trees. No crime committed, just a mystery
that Joe had to fathom. Hand on shoulder holster, he began running.

Behind the windows of morning, two bodies, brown and white,
watched from a curtained apartment, their flesh slanted with light.
In parks greying into dawn, doves flocked into trees black
with starlings, white bird between each black one. Looking back
over her shoulder, Emen stared down at the immense crowd
gathering by the empty band shell and she smiled. At her back
Will smiled too and checked his watch. The cops with their light
automatics surrounded the foot of the stage along with the crowd.

Through curtained apartments linking their naked arms, our hopes
of union pass in their poverty; they gaze down at the lightening slopes
of the park, at this moment's assembly, this vaporous moment caught
between night and day, where goodness might reign in mid-thought,
in the voodooed mid-thought, if we could only get it, something primitive
to our sophistications, a susurrus in the peoples, an instant taut
with knowledge of poverty: our hopes gaze down as the popes
gaze down at Vatican Square, not in majesty, something more primitive

in the soul. Emen knew they could never get it for more than this
moment: too much at stake in ordinary lives: a child is
a future to pay for continently, a morality to hand on, and it seems
that an income measures hard work and sobriety. These are dreams
masquerading as real, the only real, and we vote for them, despite
their final cost to global peace – make no mistake, the extremes
of war and pollution stem from the most ordinary moralities:
decency, wanting to be prosperous, builds hell in heaven's despite.

In the park everything hung on a thread, the hour thunderous,
the thread extending heavenwards from the bandshell to dark clouds,
the stage empty except for some public address speakers, relic
it seemed from a previous Sunday's festival. And then on the tick
of eight, the speakers crackled and out came the electronic voice
of Hooman, piercingly artificial. (Emen had gone suddenly frantic
up in her apartment and, loa-ridden, swooned.) In the park the vast crowds
pressed Joe on all sides; he had nothing to shoot but an electronic voice.

'District A1,' came that sing-song, inhuman tone of Hooman,
'in your secret assemblies you have chosen the names of two women
to bear high office in the new-formed Union of States, this gathering
being its commencement, a reform of a nation's corruption to the furthering
of international sanity. Your task this morning is to say 'Amen'
to the reading of names, if you so will it.' At that a feathering
of doves flew from branches of trees, and the starlings joined them
on the lawns of Prospect Park, and the poem restarts: 'Amen!

and Amen!' for here came the reading of names. 'As your President,'
said Hooman's voice, 'you have chosen one name only, but consent
must now be given. Emen Penniless is that name.' And 'Amen!'
came a huge roar. 'For Vice-President, you chose Dolores –' And 'Amen!'
came that roar at the very Christian name. The voice finished,
'– Esteves.' 'Amen!' came once more, followed by a cheer. And then
everyone turned and ran for it, the cops gazing in amazement
and Joe himself spun round by racing bodies. It had finished

in seconds. A muffled boom from under the band stage indicated
the equipment had auto-destructed in Spirit fashion: what is stated
lasts for a breath, but Spirit endures for ever. By 8 oh 5
the park was cleared, whole families hurrying along streets alive
with laughter, and twenty or so of the ordinary voters held
by the cops – but who had shouted what? No one could ever prove
anything. Spirit's leaders had been absent; the crowd had created
a new U.S.A. in a park: that was the district their 'Union' now held.

CODA

What was promised has been performed. The Penniless couple have begun
a new path on rough ground. Emen is president of the one
district fit to be united, to be a state. All has happened in a breath
and now it has ended, not a trace left behind. Why this death
of the so-newly-born? Well, follow the brief sequel and you'll understand.
The Feds tried to find charges, but so little had happened they had weft
without woof; the evidence unraveled, everything came undone.
Lou on tax crimes: small, a fine – as I expect you'll understand,

he'd sort of confessed by leaving the clues for Joe's Spiritgate
team. The others, a day or two in jug, an attempt to slate
Emen for that misprision charge – fizzled out. The reader has been had,
evidently, by the poet (by Will?). Well, it's who's has had
who? The story built nationally for a month – most racist headline:
'The Black Confederates of District A1'. 'The Secession of the Hundred
Thousand' read the *Post* in the usual media attempt to inflate
collapsing news. Is that what it comes to? A mere headline?

It all flickered on for a year. Lightning elections were staged
in other states like old-time prize fights while authorities raged
to see evidence vanish away. The wall of women became
world famous as a political tactic; versions of the drug scam
cropped up; neighborhoods were being bought up somewhat more than before;
High John was a legend; national election turnouts – already a shame-
ful statistic – worsened. All too soon, Spirit seemed to have aged.
As it does: it can never breathe for more than a moment before

a poem is finished. What did you expect? You, hypocrite reader,
et cetera? You want some opiate, a poetic abracadabra
so your ordinary responsibility for our ordinary political failure
can be charmed away? No. America, that jackass soiled with its ordure
its continued braying of freedom, knows half its own people
block their ears and don't vote. Take case. Suppose a peculiar
political wind blew, and a plebiscite – to decide whether a
new Constitution like Spirit's was acceptable to the people –

should be nationally staged by some worst U.S. president – Johnson
or Nixon or Reagan or Bush or Kennedy, all of them poison
and stained with death. Just the one proposal, to prevent the waste
of world oil by cutting out private cars, would suffice for the rest
of the changes not to be listened to, for it scarcely requires astute
judgment to see the consequent recession, massive job loss, the unrest
in manufacturing industry, the crash on Wall Street, and so on.
Not to mention the other proposals whose drawbacks those scarcely astute

minds can equally easily plumb: the leveling of income
('theft'), a Great Power fallen powerless when war has become
an individual matter of choice in its people. The people don't vote
agreed. The people don't vote all right. They let dangerous men float
into office on a flotsam tide of neglect – themselves still decent,
unresponsible for genocide and globicide. 'Free.' So suppose a turnout
of 70% – virtually unprecedented this century – everyone from the bum
to the wealthiest GOP, from Mafia riff-raff to the sober and decent,

voting whether to enter national poverty. We imagine it turned down
overwhelmingly. Ah! Search the past for the most ancient wisdom
in the world: that too much possession, too great a seeking of thrill,
harms the soul! Are all the saints and saintesses who fill
the sacred pages of myth simply wrong? Can science, another jackass,
be braying Final Truth? We walk, 20th-century-blind, towards burial,
pretending that all will come right in some personal heavenly kingdom.
We wouldn't know Spirit if, Spirit on top, it fucked us up the ass.

Douglas Oliver was born in 1937 in Hampshire, of Scottish stock. He has been a journalist and a lecturer and is well-known in Europe and America as a performer of his own poetry. In the States, while living on New York's Lower East Side (where *Penniless Politics* was born), he taught in New York, New Jersey and Baltimore, as a visiting poet at the Naropa Institute, Colorado, and worked secretarially in a cancer hospital. Married to the American poet Alice Notley, he now teaches at the British Institute in Paris.

Douglas Oliver has published seven other books of poetry. His collected poems, *Kind* (Allardyce, Barnett, 1987), was Peter Ackroyd's choice as poetry book of the year in *The Times*' Christmas Book Supplement for 1987. His Paladin selection of poetry and prose, *Three Variations on the Theme of Harm* (1990), includes his much-praised satire on modern Britain, *The Infant and the Pearl,* a revised version of his novel, *The Harmless Building,* and a new work, *An Island That Is All the World.* His critical book *Poetry and Narrative in Performance* (Macmillan/St Martins, 1989) is a study of poetic prosody and its links with the mental experience of reading narrative fiction.

Much of his work was for a long time only available from small presses, receiving critical acclaim unusual for such fugitive publications. First published in 1991 – under Iain Sinclair's Hoarse Commerce imprint – his book-length satirical poem *Penniless Politics* appeared in a new edition from Bloodaxe Books in 1994.